Sensory Integratio for Kids with Autisn Asperger's

MW00890844

Disclaimer :
This book is intended as a supplemental guide for parents and caregivers to engage their children in Sensory Integration Therapy at home. It is not a substitute for professional therapy or medical advice. While the activities in this book can support your child's development, they are not designed to replace the individualized treatment plans provided by licensed therapists, occupational therapists, or healthcare professionals. For personalized guidance and professional evaluation, please consult with a qualified therapist or medical professional. Always follow the advice of your healthcare provider regarding your child's specific needs.

Sensory Integration Therapy involves engaging children in activities that are designed to stimulate their senses in a structured, repetitive way. These activities can help children with autism spectrum disorder (ASD) who have sensory processing issues respond more effectively to sensory input from their environment. Here are some ideas for Sensory Integration Therapy activities:

1. **Swinging and Spinning Activities**:
   - **Therapy Swings**: Use different types of swings (platform, hammock, or tire swings) to provide vestibular input. Swinging back and forth can be calming, while spinning can be alerting.
   - **Sit and Spin Toys**: Encourage the child to spin themselves, which can help with balance and spatial orientation.
2. **Deep Pressure and Proprioceptive Input**:
   - **Weighted Blankets or Vests**: Provide a sense of security and can be calming.
   - **Body Socks**: Stretchy fabric suits that provide resistance and deep pressure when the child moves.
   - **Bear Hugs or Squeezing Activities**: Gentle compression can help the child become more aware of their body.

3. **Obstacle Courses**:
    - **Indoor or Outdoor Setups**: Create courses that involve crawling under tunnels, jumping over hurdles, balancing on beams, and climbing.
    - **Sequential Tasks**: Incorporate activities that require planning and sequencing to enhance motor planning skills.
4. **Sensory Bins and Tactile Exploration**:
    - **Texture Bins**: Fill containers with sand, rice, beans, water beads, or kinetic sand for tactile exploration.
    - **Hidden Objects Game**: Hide small toys or letters in the bins for the child to find.
5. **Water Play**:
    - **Splash Tables**: Allow the child to pour, splash, and play with water to receive tactile and proprioceptive input.
    - **Bath Time Activities**: Use different temperatures, bubbles, or bath paints to enhance sensory experiences.
6. **Messy Play**:
    - **Finger Painting**: Use paints, shaving cream, or pudding to draw and write, stimulating tactile senses.
    - **Mud Kitchens**: Outdoor play involving mud can be highly engaging and beneficial.
7. **Balance and Coordination Exercises**:
    - **Balance Beams or Stepping Stones**: Improve balance and spatial awareness.
    - **Yoga Poses**: Child-friendly yoga can enhance body awareness and coordination.
8. **Fine Motor Skill Activities**:
    - **Playdough Manipulation**: Rolling, squeezing, and molding can strengthen hand muscles.
    - **Beading and Lacing**: Improves hand-eye coordination and fine motor skills.
9. **Auditory Stimulation**:
    - **Musical Instruments**: Drums, bells, or shakers can provide auditory input and improve rhythm.
    - **Sound Matching Games**: Identify different sounds to enhance auditory discrimination.
10. **Visual Motor Activities**:
    - **Light Tables**: Use transparent or translucent objects on a light table to stimulate visual senses.
    - **Puzzles and Pattern Games**: Enhance visual perception and cognitive skills.
11. **Oral Motor Activities**:

- **Chewing Toys or Foods**: Items that are safe to chew can provide proprioceptive input to the mouth.
- **Blowing Bubbles or Whistles**: Strengthen oral muscles and improve breath control.

2. **Heavy Work Activities**:
   - **Pushing or Pulling**: Have the child push a weighted cart or pull a wagon.
   - **Carrying Objects**: Encourage carrying books or groceries (appropriate to their strength) to provide proprioceptive input.

3. **Sensory Diets**:
   - **Scheduled Sensory Breaks**: Incorporate short, regular intervals of sensory activities throughout the day.
   - **Customized Activities**: Tailor activities to the child's specific sensory needs (e.g., calming activities when overstimulated).

14. **Joint Compression and Stretching**:
   - **Therapeutic Exercises**: Simple stretches or compressions can help with proprioception.
   - **Animal Walks**: Encourage movements like crab walks, bear crawls, or frog jumps.

15. **Taste and Smell Exploration**:
   - **Scented Playdough**: Use different scents to stimulate olfactory senses.
   - **Taste Tests**: Introduce various flavors and textures in foods to explore taste senses.

16. **Visual Tracking Exercises**:
   - **Flashlight Tag**: Use a flashlight in a dark room for the child to follow.
   - **Bubble Gazing**: Watch and track bubbles as they float and pop.

17. **Social Sensory Activities**:
   - **Group Games**: Play games that involve turn-taking and cooperation to develop social skills alongside sensory input.
   - **Dance and Movement**: Encourage dancing to music to integrate auditory and movement senses.

18. **Therapeutic Listening Programs**:
   - **Music Therapy**: Use specific music or sounds to help with auditory processing.
   - **Environmental Sounds**: Gradually introduce sounds from everyday environments to reduce sensitivity.

19. **Sensory-Friendly Crafts**:
   - **Collage Making**: Use materials of different textures like feathers, sandpaper, or fabrics.
   - **Building Blocks**: Playing with blocks of various sizes and weights can provide tactile and proprioceptive input.

20. **Environmental Modifications**:
   - **Sensory Rooms or Corners**: Create a dedicated space with controlled sensory input (e.g., soft lighting, calming sounds).
   - **Adjustable Lighting**: Use dimmers or coloured lights to create different visual stimuli.

Tips for Implementing Sensory Integration Activities:

- **Consult a Professional**: Work with an occupational therapist trained in sensory integration to create a personalized program.
- **Start Slowly**: Introduce new activities gradually to monitor the child's response.
- **Observe and Adapt**: Pay attention to the child's cues; if an activity is overwhelming, adjust accordingly.
- **Safety First**: Ensure that all equipment and activities are safe and appropriate for the child's age and abilities.
- **Engage the Child's Interests**: Incorporate themes or items the child enjoys to increase engagement.
- **Consistency**: Regular practice can lead to better outcomes over time.
- **Parental Involvement**: Parents can reinforce activities at home to provide consistent sensory experiences.

Important Considerations:

- **Individual Differences**: Every child with autism is unique, and what is stimulating for one child may be overwhelming for another.
- **Sensory Overload**: Be cautious of overstimulation; signs include increased anxiety, irritability, or withdrawal.
- **Integration into Daily Routines**: Incorporate sensory activities into everyday life to make them more natural and less intrusive.

By incorporating these activities into therapy sessions or daily routines, children with autism can improve their ability to process sensory information, which may enhance their overall functioning and quality of life. Always tailor activities to the individual needs of the child and seek professional guidance to ensure the most effective and safe approach.

Let's go through all the Activities one by one

1. Sensory Treasure Hunt

Embark on a **Sensory Treasure Hunt** right in your living room or backyard! This engaging activity involves hiding a variety of textured items for your child to find and explore. From soft cotton balls to rough sandpaper, the goal is to create a fun-filled adventure that stimulates multiple senses. The treasure hunt can be themed around pirates searching for treasure, explorers on a mission, or any storyline that captivates your child's imagination.

How It's Done:

1. **Gather a Variety of Textured Items**: Collect objects with different textures—smooth stones, fuzzy fabrics, squishy stress balls, crunchy leaves, etc.
2. **Hide the Items**: Place these items around the designated play area. Ensure they are hidden but still accessible and safe to find.
3. **Create a Map or Clues**: Depending on your child's age and reading ability, you can create a simple map or provide verbal clues to lead them to the treasures.
4. **Begin the Hunt**: Encourage your child to find all the hidden items. As they find each one, discuss how it feels, sounds, or even smells.
5. **Sensory Exploration**: After all treasures are found, spend time exploring each item's sensory properties together.

Benefits:

- **Enhances Sensory Processing Skills**: Helps children become more comfortable with different textures and sensations.
- **Promotes Fine Motor Skills**: Picking up and handling various objects improves dexterity.
- **Encourages Problem-Solving**: Following clues or a map boosts cognitive development.
- **Boosts Communication**: Discussing each item can enhance vocabulary and expressive language.
- **Fun Physical Activity**: Keeps kids active and engaged, which is beneficial for overall health.

Toys and Tools Used:

- **Textured Items**: Cotton balls, sandpaper pieces, smooth stones, fuzzy fabric scraps, squishy toys, etc.
- **Map or Clues**: Handmade treasure map, picture clues, or verbal instructions.
- **Storage Container**: A treasure chest or box to collect found items.
- **Optional Props**: Pirate hats, explorer vests, or magnifying glasses to enhance the theme.

Goals

- Sensory treasure hunt for kids with autism
- Engaging sensory activities for ADHD
- Fun at-home sensory play ideas
- Autism-friendly treasure hunt game
- Sensory processing activities for children
- DIY sensory exploration for Asperger's
- Interactive sensory games for kids
- Fine motor skill activities for autism
- Problem-solving games for children with ADHD
- Textured sensory play ideas at home

By incorporating a **Sensory Treasure Hunt** into your child's playtime, you're not only providing an enjoyable experience but also supporting their sensory development in a natural, engaging way. This activity is easy to set up, customizable to your child's interests, and can be a delightful adventure for the whole family.

2. Bubble Wrap Stomp

The **Bubble Wrap Stomp** is an exhilarating activity where kids get to jump, dance, and stomp on bubble wrap spread out on the floor. This simple yet highly stimulating exercise provides auditory, tactile, and proprioceptive input, making it ideal for children with sensory processing needs. The joy of hearing the pops underfoot while feeling the bubbles burst adds layers of sensory feedback that can be both exciting and calming.

How It's Done:

1. **Prepare the Area**: Clear a safe, open space free of obstacles.

2. **Lay Out Bubble Wrap**: Spread large sheets of bubble wrap on the floor. Secure them with tape to prevent slipping.
3. **Set the Stage**: You can play upbeat music to encourage movement or keep it quiet to focus on the sounds of the popping bubbles.
4. **Begin Stomping**: Invite your child to walk, jump, or dance on the bubble wrap. Encourage different movements like tiptoeing or hopping.
5. **Interactive Play**: Join in the fun or create games like "Pop all the bubbles before the song ends."

Benefits:

- **Sensory Stimulation**: Provides tactile feedback from the bubble wrap and auditory input from the popping sounds.
- **Gross Motor Skills Development**: Enhances coordination, balance, and body awareness through movement.
- **Energy Release**: Great for kids with high energy levels, helping them to focus better afterward.
- **Emotional Regulation**: Can be calming for some children, reducing anxiety and stress.
- **Social Interaction**: If played in groups, it promotes sharing and cooperative play.

Toys and Tools Used:

- **Bubble Wrap Sheets**: Available from packaging stores or online.
- **Tape**: To secure bubble wrap to the floor.
- **Music Player**: Optional, for playing songs to dance along to.
- **Comfortable Footwear**: Or the activity can be done barefoot if safe and comfortable.

Goals

- Bubble wrap stomp activity for autism
- Sensory play with bubble wrap for kids
- Gross motor activities for children with ADHD
- Fun tactile sensory games at home
- Proprioceptive input activities for Asperger's
- Energy-burning activities for hyperactive kids
- Auditory stimulation games for autism
- Bubble wrap dance party for sensory processing
- Calming activities for anxious children
- Indoor movement games for kids with ADHD

The **Bubble Wrap Stomp** is a fantastic way to combine fun and therapeutic benefits. It's an activity that can be easily set up at home and adjusted to suit your child's preferences and needs. Whether it's a rainy day indoors or a scheduled sensory break, this activity is sure to bring joy and valuable sensory input.

3. Homemade Sensory Bottles

Creating **Homemade Sensory Bottles** is a calming and visually stimulating activity that involves filling clear bottles with various materials like glitter, beads, or coloured water. These bottles can be shaken, rolled, or simply observed, providing a soothing experience that can help children self-regulate their emotions. Making the bottles can be an engaging craft project, and using them offers ongoing sensory benefits.

How It's Done:

1. **Gather Materials**: Collect clear plastic bottles, glitter, beads, food colouring, water, oil, small toys, sequins, etc.
2. **Fill the Bottles**: Let your child choose and add materials to the bottles. For example:
   - **Calm Down Bottle**: Fill with water, glitter glue, and a few drops of food colouring.
   - **I-Spy Bottle**: Fill with rice and small objects or letters to find.
3. **Seal the Bottles**: Secure the lids tightly using glue or tape to prevent leaks.
4. **Explore**: Shake or turn the bottles and watch how the contents move.
5. **Use for Relaxation**: Encourage your child to use the bottles during quiet time or when they need to calm down.

Benefits:

- **Visual Stimulation**: Watching the movement inside the bottle can be mesmerizing and soothing.
- **Fine Motor Skills**: Filling the bottles helps develop hand-eye coordination.
- **Emotional Regulation**: Provides a tool for managing stress or overwhelming feelings.
- **Creativity and Choice**: Allows children to make decisions and express preferences.

- **Focus and Attention**: Helps improve concentration as they observe the contents settling.

Toys and Tools Used:

- **Clear Plastic Bottles**: Recycled water bottles or specialty craft bottles.
- **Fillers**: Glitter, beads, sequins, coloured sand, small toys, etc.
- **Liquids**: Water, clear glue, baby oil, or glycerin.
- **Adhesives**: Super glue or strong tape to seal lids.
- **Optional Decorations**: Stickers or markers to personalize the bottles.

Goals

- DIY sensory bottles for kids with autism
- Calming sensory activities for ADHD
- How to make sensory bottles at home
- Visual stimulation tools for Asperger's
- Emotional regulation techniques for children
- Craft activities for kids with autism
- Fine motor skills development with sensory bottles
- Homemade calming jars for children
- Sensory processing toys for ADHD
- Focus enhancement activities for kids

Homemade Sensory Bottles offer a simple yet effective way to provide ongoing sensory input. They're portable, customizable, and can become a cherished tool in your child's sensory toolbox. Plus, the process of making them adds an extra layer of engagement and fun.

4. Finger Painting Fun

Dive into the colourful world of **Finger Painting Fun**, where kids can express themselves freely while experiencing different textures and sensations. This hands-on activity allows children to create art using their fingers, hands, or even feet, promoting tactile exploration and creativity. It's messy, it's exciting, and it's an excellent way for kids to connect with their senses.

How It's Done:

1. **Set Up the Space**: Cover a table or floor area with a plastic sheet or newspapers to protect surfaces.
2. **Prepare the Materials**: Provide non-toxic, washable finger paints in various colours and large sheets of paper or canvas.
3. **Encourage Exploration**: Invite your child to dip their fingers or hands into the paint and create whatever they like.
4. **Discuss Textures and Colours**: Talk about how the paint feels—is it cold, slimy, smooth?
5. **Create Together**: Join in the fun to make it a shared experience.
6. **Clean Up**: Have warm soapy water and towels ready for easy cleanup afterward.

Benefits:

- **Sensory Stimulation**: Engages the tactile senses through direct contact with different textures.
- **Enhances Creativity**: Encourages self-expression and imagination.
- **Improves Fine Motor Skills**: Manipulating paint helps develop hand and finger strength.
- **Emotional Expression**: Allows children to express feelings non-verbally.
- **Colour Recognition**: Helps in learning and identifying different colours.

Toys and Tools Used:

- **Finger Paints**: Non-toxic, washable varieties are best.
- **Paper or Canvas**: Large sheets to give ample space for creativity.
- **Protective Coverings**: Tablecloths, newspapers, or plastic sheets.
- **Aprons or Old Clothes**: To keep clothing clean.
- **Cleaning Supplies**: Warm water, soap, and towels.

Goals

- Finger painting activities for kids with autism
- Tactile sensory play for ADHD
- Creative art therapy for children with Asperger's
- Messy play ideas for sensory development
- Fine motor skill activities with finger paints
- Emotional expression through art for kids
- Colour recognition games for children
- Sensory-friendly art projects at home
- Non-verbal communication activities for autism
- How to set up finger painting for kids

Finger Painting Fun is more than just an art project; it's a multi-sensory experience that can be both therapeutic and enjoyable. Embrace the mess and watch your child explore their creativity while reaping numerous developmental benefits.

---

5. Sensory Storytime

Sensory Storytime transforms traditional reading sessions into interactive adventures by incorporating tactile objects, sounds, smells, and movements related to the story. This immersive approach makes stories come alive, capturing the attention of children with autism, ADHD, or Asperger's. It's a fantastic way to enhance comprehension, engagement, and enjoyment of books.

How It's Done:

1. **Choose an Engaging Book**: Select a story rich in descriptive language and sensory elements.
2. **Gather Props**: Collect items that relate to the story—soft fabrics, toy animals, musical instruments, scented objects, etc.
3. **Interactive Reading**: As you read, encourage your child to touch, smell, or interact with the props when they appear in the story.
4. **Add Movements and Sounds**: Incorporate actions like jumping, clapping, or making sound effects to match the narrative.
5. **Discuss the Story**: Ask open-ended questions to promote comprehension and communication.

Benefits:

- **Enhances Sensory Integration**: Engages multiple senses simultaneously.
- **Improves Listening Skills**: Keeps children attentive and focused.
- **Boosts Language Development**: Expands vocabulary and understanding of language.
- **Encourages Imagination**: Brings stories to life, fostering creativity.
- **Strengthens Bonding**: Shared activity enhances connection between child and reader.

Toys and Tools Used:

- **Books**: Preferably with rich sensory descriptions.

- **Props**: Relevant to the story—textures, scents, sounds.
- **Audio Aids**: Sound effect devices or musical instruments.
- **Visual Aids**: Pictures or flashcards illustrating story elements.
- **Comfortable Reading Space**: Cozy area free from distractions.

Goals

- Sensory storytime ideas for autism
- Interactive reading activities for kids with ADHD
- Enhancing comprehension through sensory play
- Language development games for children with Asperger's
- Multi-sensory storytelling techniques
- Engaging books for sensory integration
- Improving focus with interactive storytime
- Props for sensory reading sessions
- Boosting imagination in kids with autism
- Parent-child bonding activities through reading

Sensory Storytime turns reading into a dynamic experience that can significantly benefit children with sensory processing challenges. By involving their senses, you're helping them connect more deeply with the material, making reading both fun and educational.

---

6. Play Dough Sculpting

Play Dough Sculpting is a hands-on activity where children use play dough to create shapes, figures, or anything their imagination conjures. This tactile experience engages their sense of touch and boosts creativity.

How It's Done:

1. **Set Up the Workspace**: Cover a table with a mat or cloth for easy cleanup.
2. **Provide Play Dough**: Offer various colours of non-toxic play dough.
3. **Introduce Tools**: Include cookie cutters, rolling pins, and plastic utensils.
4. **Encourage Creation**: Let your child mold and shape the dough freely.
5. **Discuss Textures and Shapes**: Talk about how the dough feels and the forms they're making.

Benefits:

- **Enhances Fine Motor Skills**: Manipulating dough strengthens hand muscles.
- **Stimulates Tactile Senses**: Direct contact with the dough provides rich sensory input.
- **Encourages Creativity**: Fosters imaginative play and expression.
- **Improves Focus**: Concentrating on sculpting can increase attention span.
- **Emotional Expression**: Offers a medium for expressing feelings non-verbally.

Toys and Tools Used:

- **Non-Toxic Play Dough**: Store-bought or homemade.
- **Sculpting Tools**: Plastic knives, cookie cutters, rolling pins.
- **Accessories**: Beads, buttons, or sticks to decorate creations.
- **Protective Covering**: Tablecloth or mat for easy cleanup.

Goals

- Play dough activities for kids with autism
- Fine motor skill development with sculpting
- Tactile sensory play for ADHD children
- Creative expression through play dough
- Hands-on activities for Asperger's syndrome
- Improving focus with sculpting activities
- Non-toxic play dough ideas at home
- Enhancing creativity in children with autism
- Sensory integration through molding and shaping
- Emotional expression using play dough

---

7. Sensory Obstacle Course

Create a **Sensory Obstacle Course** that combines physical challenges with sensory experiences. This dynamic activity engages multiple senses and encourages gross motor skill development.

How It's Done:

1. **Design the Course**: Use pillows, tunnels, balance beams, and textured mats.

2. **Set Up Stations**: Each station offers a different sensory input (e.g., crawling under a blanket fort, walking over bubble wrap).
3. **Explain the Course**: Walk your child through each obstacle.
4. **Encourage Participation**: Let them navigate the course at their own pace.
5. **Repeat and Modify**: Adjust obstacles based on your child's comfort level.

Benefits:

- **Enhances Gross Motor Skills**: Improves coordination and balance.
- **Provides Sensory Input**: Engages tactile, proprioceptive, and vestibular senses.
- **Boosts Confidence**: Completing the course can increase self-esteem.
- **Encourages Problem-Solving**: Navigating obstacles develops cognitive skills.
- **Physical Exercise**: Promotes overall health and well-being.

Toys and Tools Used:

- **Household Items**: Pillows, blankets, chairs.
- **Sensory Materials**: Bubble wrap, textured mats.
- **Play Equipment**: Tunnels, balance beams (can be homemade).
- **Safety Gear**: Soft padding where necessary.

Goals

- Sensory obstacle course ideas for autism
- Gross motor activities for ADHD kids
- Indoor physical activities for children with Asperger's
- DIY obstacle course at home
- Proprioceptive and vestibular sensory play
- Confidence-building activities for kids
- Problem-solving games for children with autism
- Engaging physical exercises for ADHD
- Sensory integration through obstacle courses
- Fun indoor activities for sensory development

8. Aromatherapy Playtime

Introduce **Aromatherapy Playtime** by using scented play dough or essential oils to engage your child's sense of smell. This activity can be both stimulating and calming, depending on the scents used.

How It's Done:

1. **Choose Safe Scents**: Select child-safe essential oils like lavender or citrus.
2. **Scented Materials**: Add a few drops to play dough, slime, or cotton balls.
3. **Explore the Scents**: Encourage your child to smell and describe the aromas.
4. **Incorporate into Play**: Use scented items during regular play activities.
5. **Observe Reactions**: Note which scents your child enjoys or finds calming.

Benefits:

- **Stimulates Olfactory Sense**: Engages the sense of smell in a safe way.
- **Calming Effect**: Certain scents can reduce anxiety and promote relaxation.
- **Enhances Emotional Awareness**: Helps children recognize how different smells affect their mood.
- **Encourages Descriptive Language**: Discussing scents can expand vocabulary.
- **Supports Sensory Integration**: Combines smell with touch and sight during play.

Toys and Tools Used:

- **Essential Oils**: Child-safe options like lavender, orange, or peppermint.
- **Base Materials**: Unscented play dough, slime, or water beads.
- **Containers**: Small jars or sensory bottles for holding scented items.
- **Safety Supplies**: Towels and soap for cleaning up.

Goals

- Aromatherapy activities for kids with autism
- Scent-based sensory play for ADHD children
- Calming scents for children with Asperger's
- Using essential oils in sensory activities
- Olfactory stimulation games at home
- Relaxation techniques for kids with autism
- Emotional awareness through aromatherapy

- Scented play dough recipes
- Sensory integration with smells
- Enhancing mood with aromatherapy play

9. Texture Touch Boards

Create **Texture Touch Boards** by assembling a variety of materials with different textures on a board. This tactile activity helps children become more comfortable with touching various surfaces.

How It's Done:

1. **Gather Materials**: Collect fabrics and items like sandpaper, velvet, fur, bubble wrap, and felt.
2. **Prepare the Board**: Use a sturdy piece of cardboard or foam board.
3. **Attach Textures**: Glue or tape each material onto the board in sections.
4. **Explore Together**: Encourage your child to touch each texture and describe how it feels.
5. **Incorporate into Play**: Use the board during storytime or as a calming tool.

Benefits:

- **Enhances Tactile Exploration**: Introduces a range of textures in a controlled way.
- **Improves Sensory Processing**: Helps desensitize aversions to certain textures.
- **Builds Vocabulary**: Describing textures expands language skills.
- **Portable Sensory Tool**: Easy to take along for on-the-go sensory breaks.
- **Customizable**: Tailor the textures to your child's preferences or needs.

Toys and Tools Used:

- **Base Board**: Cardboard, foam board, or wood.
- **Textured Materials**: Fabrics, sandpaper, foam, bubble wrap.
- **Adhesives**: Glue, tape, or Velcro.
- **Decorative Items**: Stickers or markers to personalize the board.

Goals

- Texture touch boards for autism therapy
- DIY tactile sensory boards for kids
- Sensory processing activities for ADHD
- Exploring textures with children
- Building tactile tolerance in kids with Asperger's
- Language development through sensory play
- Portable sensory tools for autism
- Customizable tactile activities at home
- Describing textures to enhance vocabulary
- Sensory integration using touch boards

10. Musical Instrument Exploration

Allow your child to discover sounds through **Musical Instrument Exploration**. This auditory activity involves playing with various instruments to create and listen to different sounds.

How It's Done:

1. **Collect Instruments**: Use drums, xylophones, shakers, bells, or homemade instruments.
2. **Create a Music Space**: Set up an area where noise is acceptable.
3. **Free Play**: Let your child experiment with making sounds.
4. **Structured Activities**: Introduce simple rhythms or songs to mimic.
5. **Discuss Sounds**: Talk about loud vs. soft, high vs. low pitches.

Benefits:

- **Auditory Stimulation**: Engages the sense of hearing in a fun way.
- **Fine and Gross Motor Skills**: Playing instruments enhances coordination.
- **Emotional Expression**: Music can be a medium for expressing feelings.
- **Cognitive Development**: Understanding rhythms and patterns boosts brain development.
- **Cultural Exposure**: Introduces music from different cultures if varied instruments are used.

Toys and Tools Used:

- **Musical Instruments**: Both real and homemade options.

- **Homemade Options**: Pots and pans, rice shakers, rubber band guitars.
- **Music Area Setup**: Comfortable seating or standing space.
- **Recording Device**: Optional, to play back and listen.

Goals

- Musical activities for kids with autism
- Auditory sensory play for ADHD children
- Exploring sounds with musical instruments
- Fine motor skills through instrument play
- Emotional expression using music for Asperger's
- Homemade musical instruments for kids
- Cognitive development with music activities
- Cultural learning through music exploration
- Sound discrimination games for children
- Sensory integration using auditory stimuli

I understand that you need a comprehensive list of 200 sensory activities with detailed descriptions. Providing all of them in this format would be quite extensive for a single response. To ensure I assist you effectively, perhaps we can focus on generating a specific number of activities at a time or concentrate on particular categories. Please let me know how you'd like to proceed, and I'll be happy to help further.

Certainly, let's continue with more sensory activities for your book. I'll provide detailed descriptions, how to conduct each activity, the benefits, and the tools needed, all in an engaging, conversational tone with SEO-friendly keywords.

---

11. Bubble Blowing Bonanza

Dive into a world of shimmering bubbles with the **Bubble Blowing Bonanza**! This activity involves blowing bubbles using wands of various shapes and sizes. It's a delightful way to engage children's visual tracking, oral motor skills, and sensory processing as they watch bubbles float and pop.

How It's Done:

1. **Prepare the Bubble Solution**: Use a store-bought solution or make your own by mixing water with dish soap and a bit of glycerin.
2. **Select Bubble Wands**: Provide wands of different shapes and sizes, or make your own using pipe cleaners or straws.
3. **Blowing Bubbles**: Show your child how to dip the wand and gently blow to create bubbles.
4. **Chase and Pop**: Encourage them to chase the bubbles and pop them using different parts of their body—fingers, elbows, or even noses!
5. **Experiment**: Try waving the wand or using a bubble machine for continuous bubbles.

Benefits:

- **Oral Motor Development**: Blowing bubbles strengthens mouth and jaw muscles.
- **Visual Tracking Skills**: Following bubbles with their eyes enhances focus and coordination.
- **Gross Motor Skills**: Chasing bubbles encourages movement and physical activity.
- **Sensory Stimulation**: The feel of bubbles popping provides tactile feedback.
- **Emotional Joy**: Bubbles often bring smiles and laughter, boosting mood.

Toys and Tools Used:

- **Bubble Solution**: Homemade or store-bought.
- **Bubble Wands**: Various sizes and shapes.
- **DIY Wands**: Pipe cleaners, straws, or cookie cutters.
- **Bubble Machine**: Optional for continuous bubbles.
- **Cleaning Supplies**: Towels in case of spills.

Goals

- Bubble activities for kids with autism
- Oral motor skill development with bubbles
- Visual tracking exercises for ADHD children
- Fun outdoor activities for sensory stimulation
- DIY bubble solutions and wands
- Gross motor play with bubble chasing
- Sensory processing activities with bubbles
- Engaging playtime for kids with Asperger's
- Enhancing focus through bubble play
- Joyful sensory experiences for children

12. Sand Tray Adventures

Embark on **Sand Tray Adventures** where children can dig, build, and create in a tray filled with sand. This tactile activity allows for endless creativity while providing soothing sensory input.

How It's Done:

1. **Set Up the Sand Tray**: Use a large tray or shallow box and fill it with clean, fine sand.
2. **Add Tools and Toys**: Include items like small shovels, molds, toy cars, or figurines.
3. **Creative Play**: Encourage your child to draw in the sand, build mini sandcastles, or create imaginative scenes.
4. **Sensory Exploration**: Let them feel the sand with their hands or feet, noting the texture.
5. **Themed Adventures**: Incorporate themes like dinosaurs, beach trips, or construction sites.

Benefits:

- **Tactile Sensory Input**: Engages the sense of touch through different textures.
- **Fine Motor Skills**: Manipulating small objects strengthens hand coordination.
- **Imaginative Play**: Fosters creativity and storytelling.
- **Calming Effect**: The repetitive motion of moving sand can be soothing.
- **Social Skills**: If done with others, it promotes sharing and cooperation.

Toys and Tools Used:

- **Sand**: Play sand or kinetic sand for less mess.
- **Tray or Box**: Large enough for play.
- **Tools**: Shovels, rakes, molds.
- **Accessories**: Small toys, shells, stones.
- **Protective Mat**: To catch any spilled sand.

Goals

- Sand play activities for autism

- Tactile sensory experiences with sand trays
- Fine motor development in sand play
- Imaginative play ideas for kids with ADHD
- Calming sensory activities using sand
- Kinetic sand vs. regular sand for sensory play
- Cooperative play in sand tray activities
- Themed sensory trays for children
- Enhancing creativity with sand adventures
- Sensory integration through sand exploration

13. Glow-in-the-Dark Sensory Play

Light up the night with **Glow-in-the-Dark Sensory Play**! This activity uses glow sticks, fluorescent paints, and black lights to create a visually stimulating experience that captivates and soothes.

How It's Done:

1. **Prepare the Space**: Darken a room and set up black lights if available.
2. **Glow Materials**: Provide glow sticks, glow-in-the-dark paint, and fluorescent toys.
3. **Creative Expression**: Let your child paint on black paper, play with glow slime, or build with glowing blocks.
4. **Movement Activities**: Dance with glow sticks or create patterns in the air.
5. **Sensory Exploration**: Observe how colours change under black light.

Benefits:

- **Visual Sensory Stimulation**: Engages sight in a unique way.
- **Fine Motor Skills**: Painting and manipulating small items enhance coordination.
- **Encourages Movement**: Activities like dancing promote physical activity.
- **Calming Environment**: Soft glowing lights can be soothing.
- **Exploration of Cause and Effect**: Understanding how materials react under black light.

Toys and Tools Used:

- **Glow Sticks**: Various colours and sizes.
- **Fluorescent Paints**: Safe for children.
- **Black Light**: Enhances the glow effect.
- **Glowing Toys**: Balls, blocks, or slime.
- **Protective Clothing**: Old clothes or aprons.

Goals

- Glow-in-the-dark activities for kids with autism
- Visual sensory play with black lights
- Creative night-time play ideas for ADHD
- Fine motor skills with glow materials
- Calming sensory environments for children
- Exploring colours under black light
- Movement activities with glow sticks
- Sensory integration through visual stimulation
- Fun glow crafts for kids
- Cause and effect learning with glowing items

14. Nature Walk Scavenger Hunt

Take learning outdoors with a **Nature Walk Scavenger Hunt**. This activity combines physical exercise with sensory exploration as children search for items like leaves, rocks, or feathers.

How It's Done:

1. **Prepare a List**: Create a visual or written list of natural items to find.
2. **Choose a Location**: Visit a park, trail, or even your backyard.
3. **Safety First**: Go over safety rules, like staying on the path and not touching unknown plants.
4. **Begin the Hunt**: Encourage your child to use their senses to find the listed items.
5. **Discuss Findings**: Talk about the textures, colours, and smells of the items collected.

Benefits:

- **Multi-Sensory Engagement**: Uses sight, touch, smell, and hearing.
- **Physical Activity**: Walking and exploring promote fitness.

- **Connection with Nature**: Fosters appreciation for the environment.
- **Cognitive Development**: Enhances observation and identification skills.
- **Social Interaction**: If done with others, it encourages teamwork.

Toys and Tools Used:

- **Scavenger Hunt List**: With pictures for non-readers.
- **Bag or Basket**: To collect items.
- **Magnifying Glass**: For close-up observation.
- **Notebook and Pencil**: To draw or note findings.
- **Comfortable Shoes and Clothing**

Goals

- Nature scavenger hunts for autism
- Outdoor sensory activities for ADHD kids
- Multi-sensory exploration in nature
- Physical fitness through nature walks
- Environmental education for children
- Cognitive development with scavenger hunts
- Teamwork activities for kids with Asperger's
- Sensory integration outdoors
- Observational skills in nature
- Connecting children with the environment

15. Water Bead Sensory Bin

Immerse your child in a tactile wonderland with a **Water Bead Sensory Bin**. Water beads are small, squishy beads that expand in water, offering a unique texture for sensory play.

How It's Done:

1. **Prepare the Beads**: Soak water beads in water for several hours until fully expanded.
2. **Fill a Bin**: Place the hydrated beads into a large, shallow container.
3. **Add Tools and Toys**: Include scoops, cups, or small waterproof toys.
4. **Sensory Exploration**: Let your child run their hands through the beads, scoop them, or sort by colour.
5. **Supervise**: Ensure the beads are not ingested; they are not edible.

Benefits:

- **Tactile Sensory Input**: Unique texture stimulates touch.
- **Fine Motor Skills**: Scooping and transferring beads enhance coordination.
- **Colour Recognition**: Sorting beads by colour reinforces learning.
- **Calming Activity**: The feel of the beads can be soothing.
- **Imaginative Play**: Incorporate themes like "underwater world" or "treasure hunt."

Toys and Tools Used:

- **Water Beads**: Available in various colours.
- **Sensory Bin**: Large container or tub.
- **Scoops and Cups**: For pouring and transferring.
- **Small Toys**: Waterproof items like plastic fish or gems.
- **Towels**: For easy cleanup.

Goals

- Water bead sensory play for autism
- Tactile activities with water beads
- Fine motor development using sensory bins
- Colour sorting games for kids with ADHD
- Calming sensory experiences for children
- Imaginative play with water beads
- Safety tips for water bead activities
- Sensory integration through tactile play
- Underwater themed sensory bins
- Enhancing coordination with sensory beads

---

16. Mirror Movement Games

Engage in **Mirror Movement Games**, where the child mirrors your actions or vice versa. This activity promotes body awareness, motor skills, and social interaction.

How It's Done:

1. **Face Each Other**: Stand or sit opposite your child.

2. **Explain the Game**: One person leads with movements; the other imitates like a mirror.
3. **Start with Simple Movements**: Raise arms, nod head, wiggle fingers.
4. **Increase Complexity**: Incorporate facial expressions or full-body movements.
5. **Switch Roles**: Let your child lead while you mirror them.

Benefits:

- **Body Awareness**: Helps children understand how their bodies move in space.
- **Motor Skills**: Enhances coordination and control.
- **Social Skills**: Encourages eye contact and turn-taking.
- **Attention and Focus**: Requires concentration to mimic movements.
- **Emotional Connection**: Builds rapport and trust.

Toys and Tools Used:

- **None Needed**: Just a clear space to move.
- **Optional Props**: Scarves, ribbons, or balls to incorporate into movements.
- **Mirror**: Playing in front of a large mirror can add visual feedback.

Goals

- Mirror movement activities for autism
- Body awareness games for kids with ADHD
- Enhancing motor skills through imitation
- Social interaction exercises for children
- Attention-building activities for Asperger's
- Parent-child bonding through movement games
- Coordination exercises without equipment
- Fun indoor activities for sensory development
- Emotional connection through mirroring
- Eye contact improvement games for kids

17. Scent Matching Game

Test and develop your child's sense of smell with a **Scent Matching Game**. Use various scented cotton balls or containers to find matching pairs.

How It's Done:

1. **Prepare Scents**: Use essential oils, spices, or extracts on cotton balls placed in small containers.
2. **Create Pairs**: Have at least two cotton balls of each scent.
3. **Shuffle and Present**: Randomly place the containers on a table.
4. **Match the Scents**: Ask your child to sniff and find the matching pairs.
5. **Discuss Each Scent**: Talk about what the scent is and where it's commonly found.

Benefits:

- **Olfactory Sensory Development**: Enhances the sense of smell.
- **Memory and Matching Skills**: Improves cognitive abilities.
- **Language Skills**: Expands vocabulary related to scents.
- **Emotional Awareness**: Some scents can evoke feelings or memories.
- **Fun and Engaging**: A unique game that captures interest.

Toys and Tools Used:

- **Small Containers**: Opaque jars or film canisters.
- **Cotton Balls**: As scent carriers.
- **Scents**: Essential oils like vanilla, peppermint, lemon, etc.
- **Labels**: For adult reference (keep hidden from the child).

Goals

- Scent matching games for kids with autism
- Olfactory sensory activities for ADHD children
- Cognitive development through scent games
- Memory enhancement activities for kids
- Language building with scent identification
- Emotional connections through smells
- Fun matching games for sensory play
- DIY scent games at home
- Enhancing sense of smell in children
- Sensory integration using olfactory stimuli

18. Balloon Volleyball

Get moving with **Balloon Volleyball**, a fun game that involves keeping a balloon in the air. It's excellent for developing motor skills and promoting cooperative play.

How It's Done:

1. **Inflate a Balloon**: Use a medium-sized balloon.
2. **Set Up a Net**: Tie a string across two points to act as a net, or just play without one.
3. **Game Rules**: The goal is to keep the balloon from touching the ground by hitting it back and forth.
4. **Variations**: Use different body parts—hands, heads, or feet.
5. **Play Solo or with Others**: Can be played alone, with a partner, or in a group.

Benefits:

- **Gross Motor Skills**: Enhances coordination and timing.
- **Hand-Eye Coordination**: Tracking the balloon improves visual skills.
- **Physical Activity**: Encourages movement and exercise.
- **Social Interaction**: Playing with others builds teamwork.
- **Adaptable Difficulty**: Adjust the game's pace to suit your child.

Toys and Tools Used:

- **Balloon**: Latex or mylar (check for allergies).
- **Net Substitute**: String, tape line on the floor, or a sheet.
- **Open Space**: Indoor or outdoor area free of hazards.

Goals

- Balloon volleyball for autism therapy
- Gross motor activities with balloons
- Hand-eye coordination games for kids
- Physical exercise for children with ADHD
- Teamwork and social skills through play
- Indoor active games for sensory development
- Adaptable physical activities for Asperger's
- Fun movement games for kids
- Visual tracking exercises with balloons
- Energy-burning activities for children

19. Pasta Necklace Craft

Combine creativity and fine motor skills by making a **Pasta Necklace Craft**. Using various shapes of pasta and colourful dyes, children can create wearable art.

How It's Done:

1. **Colour the Pasta**: Dye pasta using food colouring and a bit of alcohol; let it dry completely.
2. **Prepare String**: Cut yarn or string to the desired necklace length.
3. **Threading**: Show your child how to thread the pasta onto the string.
4. **Pattern Making**: Encourage creating patterns with colours and shapes.
5. **Wear and Share**: Tie the ends and let them wear their creation or gift it to someone.

Benefits:

- **Fine Motor Skills**: Threading helps with hand-eye coordination.
- **Colour Recognition**: Identifying and choosing colours reinforces learning.
- **Pattern Recognition**: Creating sequences enhances cognitive skills.
- **Creativity and Self-Expression**: Designing their own jewelry fosters pride.
- **Sensory Experience**: The texture of pasta provides tactile input.

Toys and Tools Used:

- **Pasta**: Tubular shapes like penne or macaroni.
- **Food Colouring**: For dyeing pasta.
- **String or Yarn**: Thick enough for easy threading.
- **Bowls and Bags**: For colouring and drying pasta.
- **Scissors**: For cutting string.

Goals

- Pasta necklace crafts for kids with autism
- Fine motor skill development through threading
- Colour and pattern activities for ADHD children
- Creative jewelry making for kids
- Sensory crafts with pasta
- Cognitive development with pattern recognition

- Fun art projects for children with Asperger's
- DIY pasta crafts at home
- Enhancing coordination through craft activities
- Educational crafts for sensory integration

20. Emotion Charades

Help your child understand and express emotions with **Emotion Charades**. This game involves acting out feelings for others to guess, promoting emotional intelligence and empathy.

How It's Done:

1. **Prepare Emotion Cards**: Write down different emotions on cards—happy, sad, angry, surprised, etc.
2. **Explain the Game**: One person picks a card and acts out the emotion without words.
3. **Guess the Emotion**: Others try to identify the emotion being portrayed.
4. **Discuss Each Emotion**: Talk about situations that might cause these feelings.
5. **Rotate Turns**: Give everyone a chance to act and guess.

Benefits:

- **Emotional Awareness**: Recognizing and naming emotions.
- **Expressive Skills**: Encourages using body language and facial expressions.
- **Empathy Development**: Understanding how others feel.
- **Social Interaction**: Promotes turn-taking and listening.
- **Cognitive Skills**: Enhances memory and recall.

Toys and Tools Used:

- **Emotion Cards**: DIY or printable cards.
- **Space to Act**: Room to move and express.
- **Visual Aids**: Emotion charts or faces for reference.

Goals

- Emotion recognition games for autism

- Social-emotional learning activities for kids
- Enhancing empathy in children with ADHD
- Acting and role-play for emotional development
- Expressive skills through charades
- Understanding feelings for kids with Asperger's
- Fun group activities for emotional intelligence
- Non-verbal communication games
- Cognitive development with emotion games
- Teaching emotions through play

21. Ice Excavation Exploration

Embark on an icy adventure with **Ice Excavation Exploration**! Freeze small toys or objects within blocks of ice and let your child excavate them using safe tools. This activity engages the senses and introduces basic scientific concepts like states of matter.

How It's Done:

1. **Prepare the Ice Blocks:** Place small plastic toys, like dinosaurs or beads, into containers filled with water and freeze them overnight.
2. **Set Up the Excavation Site:** Remove the ice blocks from the containers and place them in a larger tray to catch melting water.
3. **Provide Tools:** Offer tools like plastic spoons, droppers with warm water, or small brushes.
4. **Begin Excavation:** Encourage your child to free the trapped objects by melting or chipping away the ice.
5. **Discuss the Process:** Talk about how ice melts and the concepts of solid and liquid states.

Benefits:

- **Tactile Sensory Input:** The cold temperature provides unique tactile stimulation.
- **Fine Motor Skills:** Manipulating tools enhances dexterity.
- **Problem-Solving Skills:** Finding effective ways to melt or break the ice promotes critical thinking.
- **Scientific Understanding:** Introduces basic science concepts in a hands-on way.

- **Prolonged Engagement:** The activity can keep children occupied and focused.

Toys and Tools Used:

- **Containers:** Ice cube trays, plastic cups, or silicone molds.
- **Small Toys:** Plastic figures, beads, or buttons.
- **Tools:** Plastic spoons, droppers, brushes.
- **Warm Water:** For melting ice.
- **Tray or Basin:** To contain water as the ice melts.

Goals

- Ice excavation activities for kids with autism
- Sensory play with ice and water
- Fine motor development through ice play
- Science experiments for children with ADHD
- Tactile sensory experiences with cold temperatures
- Problem-solving skills in sensory activities
- Engaging outdoor activities for kids
- Understanding states of matter through play
- Hands-on science for children with Asperger's
- Prolonged focus activities for sensory development

---

22. Feely Bag Guessing Game

Test and enhance your child's sense of touch with the **Feely Bag Guessing Game**. Place various objects inside an opaque bag and have your child reach in to guess what they are without looking.

How It's Done:

1. **Select Items:** Choose objects with distinct textures—like a spoon, sponge, pinecone, or toy car.
2. **Prepare the Bag:** Use a non-transparent bag or pillowcase.
3. **Explain the Game:** Tell your child they'll feel an object and try to guess what it is using only their hands.
4. **Begin Guessing:** Place one item in the bag at a time and let them explore it tactually.

5. **Reveal and Discuss:** After guessing, show the item and talk about its texture and use.

Benefits:

- **Tactile Sensory Development:** Enhances the sense of touch.
- **Descriptive Language Skills:** Encourages the use of adjectives and descriptive words.
- **Cognitive Skills:** Improves memory and object recognition.
- **Confidence Building:** Success in guessing boosts self-esteem.
- **Fun and Engaging:** Makes learning enjoyable.

Toys and Tools Used:

- **Opaque Bag:** A pillowcase or fabric bag.
- **Variety of Objects:** Items safe to touch and appropriate for your child.
- **Blindfold (Optional):** To prevent peeking.

Goals

- Feely bag games for sensory development
- Tactile guessing games for kids with autism
- Enhancing descriptive language through play
- Cognitive development with sensory activities
- Confidence-building games for children with ADHD
- Fun tactile activities for kids
- Object recognition through touch
- Sensory integration using feely bags
- Engaging indoor games for children
- Language skills enhancement for kids with Asperger's

23. Bubble Foam Sensory Play

Create a fluffy, tactile experience with **Bubble Foam Sensory Play**. This activity involves making coloured foam for children to explore, squish, and manipulate, engaging their senses in a delightful way.

How It's Done:

1. **Make the Foam:** Mix water, dish soap, and a few drops of food colouring in a bowl. Use a hand mixer or whisk to create foam.
2. **Set Up a Play Area:** Place the foam in a large bin or tray.
3. **Sensory Exploration:** Let your child dive in with their hands, toy cars, or molds.
4. **Creative Play:** Encourage making shapes, letters, or pretend baking.
5. **Clean Up:** The foam is soapy, making cleanup easy—just rinse everything off.

Benefits:

- **Tactile Stimulation:** Soft, squishy texture engages the sense of touch.
- **Fine Motor Skills:** Manipulating foam improves hand strength.
- **Colour Recognition:** Using different colours can reinforce learning.
- **Imaginative Play:** Stimulates creativity and storytelling.
- **Calming Activity:** The repetitive motion of playing with foam can be soothing.

Toys and Tools Used:

- **Ingredients:** Water, dish soap, food colouring.
- **Mixer:** Hand mixer or whisk.
- **Container:** Large bin or tray.
- **Accessories:** Molds, small toys, scoops.

Goals

- Bubble foam play for kids with autism
- Tactile sensory activities with foam
- DIY sensory materials for children
- Fine motor skill development through foam play
- Calming sensory experiences for ADHD
- Colourful sensory play ideas
- Imaginative activities with bubble foam
- Easy cleanup sensory activities
- Enhancing touch senses in children
- Indoor sensory play for kids with Asperger's

24. Auditory Memory Game

Boost auditory processing with the **Auditory Memory Game**. This activity involves listening to a sequence of sounds or words and repeating them back, enhancing listening skills and memory.

How It's Done:

1. **Prepare Sounds or Words:** Create a list of sounds using instruments or select words/themes.
2. **Explain the Game:** Tell your child you'll make sounds or say words that they need to remember and repeat.
3. **Start Simple:** Begin with a short sequence, gradually increasing the length.
4. **Use Variations:** Incorporate claps, taps, or use digital sound effects.
5. **Positive Reinforcement:** Praise efforts to encourage confidence.

Benefits:

- **Auditory Processing:** Improves the ability to interpret and remember sounds.
- **Memory Enhancement:** Strengthens short-term and working memory.
- **Attention Skills:** Increases focus and concentration.
- **Language Development:** Expands vocabulary and comprehension.
- **Fun Challenge:** Provides an engaging way to develop essential skills.

Toys and Tools Used:

- **Instruments:** Drums, bells, or shakers.
- **Sound Devices:** Apps or recordings.
- **Quiet Environment:** Minimizes distractions.

Goals

- Auditory memory games for kids with autism
- Listening skills activities for ADHD children
- Enhancing memory through sound games
- Language development with auditory exercises
- Focus and concentration games for children
- Fun auditory processing activities
- Short-term memory improvement for kids
- Sound recognition games for sensory development
- Engaging listening activities for children
- Cognitive skill enhancement through auditory play

25. Edible Finger Painting

Combine art and taste with **Edible Finger Painting**. Using food-based paints, children can create artwork and safely explore with their senses, ideal for kids who may put their hands in their mouths.

How It's Done:

1. **Prepare Edible Paints:** Mix yogurt or pudding with natural food colouring.
2. **Set Up the Canvas:** Use wax paper or a clean, flat surface.
3. **Art Creation:** Encourage your child to paint using their fingers or utensils.
4. **Sensory Exploration:** Let them taste the paints if they wish.
5. **Discuss Textures and Flavors:** Talk about how the paints feel and taste.

Benefits:

- **Safe Sensory Play:** Ideal for children who mouth objects.
- **Tactile and Taste Stimulation:** Engages multiple senses simultaneously.
- **Creativity and Expression:** Encourages artistic exploration.
- **Fine Motor Skills:** Painting motions enhance dexterity.
- **Colour Recognition:** Introduces colours in a fun way.

Toys and Tools Used:

- **Edible Paints:** Yogurt, pudding, natural food dyes.
- **Canvas:** Wax paper, plates, or baking sheets.
- **Utensils:** Spoons, brushes (if desired).

Goals

- Edible finger painting for kids with autism
- Safe sensory play with food-based paints
- Tactile and taste sensory activities
- Creative art projects for children with ADHD
- Fine motor skill development through painting
- Multisensory exploration with edible materials
- Colour learning activities for kids
- Artistic expression in sensory play
- Engaging sensory activities for toddlers
- Safe play ideas for kids who mouth objects

26. Sound Matching with Musical Bottles

Create a symphony of sounds with **Sound Matching using Musical Bottles**. Fill bottles with varying levels of water to produce different pitches, and have your child match sounds or create melodies.

How It's Done:

1. **Prepare the Bottles:** Collect several glass or plastic bottles.
2. **Fill with Water:** Add different amounts of water to each bottle.
3. **Tune the Bottles:** Tap them gently with a spoon to hear the pitches.
4. **Matching Game:** Play a note and have your child find the matching bottle.
5. **Create Music:** Encourage composing simple tunes.

Benefits:

- **Auditory Discrimination:** Enhances ability to differentiate sounds.
- **Fine Motor Skills:** Holding and tapping bottles improves coordination.
- **Introduction to Music Concepts:** Teaches pitch and tone.
- **Cognitive Development:** Supports pattern recognition.
- **Fun Experimentation:** Encourages curiosity and exploration.

Tools and Materials:

- **Bottles:** Glass for clearer sound, plastic for safety.
- **Water:** Adjust levels for different pitches.
- **Tapping Tool:** Metal or wooden spoon.

Goals

- Sound matching activities for autism
- Musical bottle games for kids
- Auditory discrimination with water bottles
- Introduction to music concepts for children
- Fine motor skills through sound play
- DIY musical instruments for sensory development
- Cognitive skills enhancement with music
- Fun sound experiments for kids with ADHD
- Engaging auditory activities for children

- Sensory integration using musical games

27. Sticky Note Wall Bop

Turn energy into fun with the **Sticky Note Wall Bop**. Write letters, numbers, or shapes on sticky notes, place them on a wall, and have your child jump or reach to grab the correct ones.

How It's Done:

1. **Prepare Sticky Notes:** Write or draw on each note.
2. **Arrange on Wall:** Place them at varying heights.
3. **Call Out Prompts:** Ask your child to find and grab specific notes.
4. **Physical Activity:** Encourage jumping, stretching, or standing on tiptoes.
5. **Celebrate Successes:** Praise efforts to boost confidence.

Benefits:

- **Gross Motor Skills:** Enhances coordination and balance.
- **Cognitive Development:** Reinforces recognition of letters, numbers, or shapes.
- **Energy Release:** Provides a physical outlet for high-energy children.
- **Listening Skills:** Follows instructions, improving attention.
- **Fun Learning:** Combines education with active play.

Tools and Materials:

- **Sticky Notes:** In bright colours.
- **Marker or Pen:** For writing or drawing.
- **Safe Wall Space:** Clear of obstacles.

Goals

- Active learning games for kids with autism
- Gross motor skill activities with sticky notes
- Letter and number recognition through play
- Energy-burning activities for ADHD children
- Listening skills enhancement in active games
- Fun educational activities for kids
- Cognitive development with movement

- Engaging wall games for sensory integration
- Confidence-building through active play
- Indoor physical activities for children

28. Texture Ball Sorting

Engage in tactile exploration with **Texture Ball Sorting**. Provide balls of different textures and have your child sort them based on how they feel.

How It's Done:

1. **Collect Balls:** Use smooth, fuzzy, spiky, and squishy balls.
2. **Set Up Bins:** Label bins or areas for each texture category.
3. **Explain the Task:** Show how to feel each ball and decide where it belongs.
4. **Sorting Activity:** Let your child sort all the balls accordingly.
5. **Discuss Textures:** Talk about the sensations each texture provides.

Benefits:

- **Tactile Sensory Development:** Enhances touch perception.
- **Categorization Skills:** Teaches grouping based on attributes.
- **Fine Motor Skills:** Handling balls improves dexterity.
- **Language Development:** Introduces descriptive words.
- **Decision Making:** Encourages independent thinking.

Tools and Materials:

- **Variety of Balls:** Different sizes and textures.
- **Sorting Bins:** Boxes or baskets.
- **Labels:** Pictures or words indicating textures.

Goals

- Texture sorting activities for autism
- Tactile sensory play with balls
- Categorization skills in children with ADHD
- Fine motor development through sorting
- Language enhancement with descriptive words
- Decision-making skills in sensory activities

- Engaging tactile games for kids
- Sensory integration using textured objects
- Fun sorting games for children
- Educational activities for touch perception

29. Rainstick Craft and Play

Create and enjoy soothing sounds with a **Rainstick Craft**. This activity involves making a rainstick using a cardboard tube and materials like rice or beans, then enjoying the auditory sensory experience.

How It's Done:

1. **Gather Materials:** Cardboard tube, aluminum foil, rice or beans, tape, and decorations.
2. **Assemble the Rainstick:** Coil the foil and insert it into the tube, seal one end, add filling, then seal the other end.
3. **Decorate:** Let your child personalize the rainstick with paints, stickers, or markers.
4. **Play the Rainstick:** Tilt it slowly to hear the sound of rain.
5. **Explore Sounds:** Experiment with different fillings for varied effects.

Benefits:

- **Auditory Sensory Input:** Provides calming, rhythmic sounds.
- **Fine Motor Skills:** Crafting enhances hand-eye coordination.
- **Creative Expression:** Decorating allows for artistic freedom.
- **Cause and Effect Understanding:** Changing tilt affects sound.
- **Cultural Education:** Introduce the rainstick's origins and uses.

Tools and Materials:

- **Cardboard Tube:** Paper towel roll.
- **Aluminum Foil:** For internal structure.
- **Fillings:** Rice, beans, lentils.
- **Decorations:** Paints, stickers, ribbons.
- **Tape or Caps:** To seal the ends.

Goals

- Rainstick crafts for kids with autism
- Auditory sensory activities with homemade instruments
- Fine motor skills through crafting
- Creative expression in sensory play
- Understanding cause and effect in children
- Calming sound activities for ADHD
- Cultural education through craft projects
- DIY musical instruments for kids
- Engaging auditory experiences for sensory development
- Artistic sensory activities for children

30. Leaf Rubbing Art

Combine nature and art with **Leaf Rubbing Art**. Collect leaves and use crayons to create rubbings, revealing the intricate patterns and promoting sensory exploration.

How It's Done:

1. **Collect Leaves:** Gather various shapes and sizes.
2. **Prepare Materials:** White paper and peeled crayons.
3. **Position Leaves:** Place a leaf underside up on a flat surface.
4. **Create Rubbing:** Lay paper over the leaf and rub the crayon gently over it.
5. **Explore and Discuss:** Talk about the different patterns and textures revealed.

Benefits:

- **Tactile Sensory Input:** Feeling leaf textures enhances touch senses.
- **Artistic Skills:** Encourages creativity and technique.
- **Nature Appreciation:** Connects children with the environment.
- **Fine Motor Skills:** Improves hand strength and control.
- **Educational Opportunity:** Learn about leaf types and plant life.

Tools and Materials:

- **Leaves:** Various types from safe plants.
- **Paper:** White drawing paper.
- **Crayons:** Peeled for side rubbing.

Goals

- Leaf rubbing art for kids with autism
- Nature-inspired sensory activities
- Fine motor development through art
- Creative outdoor activities for ADHD children
- Tactile exploration with leaves
- Educational art projects about nature
- Connecting children with the environment
- Artistic expression in sensory play
- Learning about plants through art
- Engaging craft activities for sensory integration

31. Sensory Scavenger Hunt

Embark on a thrilling **Sensory Scavenger Hunt** that transforms your home or backyard into a world of sensory exploration. This activity involves creating a list of sensory items or experiences for your child to find, touch, smell, hear, or see. It's an adventurous way to engage multiple senses while encouraging curiosity and discovery.

How It's Done:

1. **Create a Sensory List:** Compile a list of items or sensations for your child to find. For example:
   - Something soft (a plush toy)
   - A sweet scent (a flower or a scented candle)
   - A rough texture (sandpaper or a textured fabric)
   - A specific sound (a ticking clock or wind chimes)
   - Something bright red (a ball or a book cover)
2. **Hide Items or Identify Locations:** Place items around the play area or identify existing items that fit the descriptions.
3. **Provide Clues:** Depending on your child's age, you can offer simple hints or create rhymed riddles to add excitement.
4. **Begin the Hunt:** Give your child the list and encourage them to explore and find each sensory item.
5. **Explore Each Find:** When an item is found, take time to discuss it. Ask questions like, "How does it feel?" or "What do you like about this smell?"

Benefits:

- **Multi-Sensory Engagement:** Stimulates touch, sight, smell, and hearing.
- **Encourages Exploration:** Fosters a sense of adventure and curiosity.
- **Language Development:** Expands vocabulary through descriptive words.
- **Problem-Solving Skills:** Enhances cognitive abilities as they interpret clues.
- **Physical Activity:** Promotes movement and coordination.

Toys and Tools Used:

- **Household Items:** Everyday objects fitting sensory categories.
- **Clues or List:** Written descriptions or picture cards.
- **Bag or Basket:** For collecting found items.
- **Optional Rewards:** Stickers or small treats for added motivation.

To make the hunt even more engaging, consider incorporating themes like a pirate treasure hunt or a jungle expedition. You can dress up in costumes, use maps, or create simple obstacles to overcome. This not only enriches the sensory experience but also adds layers of imaginative play and storytelling.

32. Cooking and Baking Together

Step into the kitchen for a delightful sensory experience with **Cooking and Baking Together**. Preparing simple recipes allows children to touch, taste, smell, see, and hear various ingredients and cooking processes. It's a fantastic way to bond while teaching valuable life skills.

How It's Done:

1. **Choose a Simple Recipe:** Opt for child-friendly recipes like cookies, smoothies, or fruit salads.
2. **Gather Ingredients and Tools:** Prepare all necessary items, emphasizing colourful and aromatic ingredients.
3. **Involve Your Child:** Let them wash fruits, measure ingredients, mix batter, or knead dough.

4. **Discuss the Process:** Talk about textures ("How does the flour feel?"), smells ("Can you smell the vanilla?"), and sounds ("Listen to the sizzle!").
5. **Enjoy the Results:** Share the finished product together, celebrating the joint effort.

Benefits:

- **Multi-Sensory Stimulation:** Engages all five senses in a meaningful context.
- **Fine Motor Skills:** Enhances hand-eye coordination through mixing, pouring, and stirring.
- **Math and Science Skills:** Introduces measurements, counting, and observing changes.
- **Following Directions:** Improves attention and understanding of sequences.
- **Boosts Confidence:** Achieving a tasty result builds self-esteem.

Toys and Tools Used:

- **Kitchen Utensils:** Mixing bowls, measuring cups, spoons.
- **Ingredients:** Depending on the recipe—flour, fruits, chocolate chips, etc.
- **Aprons:** To make your child feel like a real chef.
- **Visual Recipe Cards:** Pictures illustrating each step can aid understanding.

Cooking together can also be an opportunity to introduce new foods and flavors in a non-pressured way, which can be particularly helpful for picky eaters. Additionally, setting the table or decorating the final dish allows for further creative expression and pride in their accomplishments.

33. Sensory Bottle Discovery

Create mesmerizing **Sensory Bottles** filled with glitter, beads, and other tiny treasures suspended in liquid. These bottles captivate with their visual appeal and soothing movement, providing a calming sensory tool that children can return to again and again.

How It's Done:

1. **Collect Clear Bottles:** Use empty plastic water bottles or specialized craft bottles.
2. **Choose Fillings:** Select a combination of glitter, sequins, small beads, buttons, or tiny toys.
3. **Prepare the Liquid:** Fill the bottle with water, clear glue, or a mixture of water and oil to adjust the flow rate of the contents.
4. **Assemble the Bottle:** Add the fillings to the bottle, then pour in the liquid. Seal the cap securely with glue to prevent leaks.
5. **Explore Together:** Shake, roll, or turn the bottle and watch the contents swirl and settle.

Benefits:

- **Visual Stimulation:** The movement and colours can be both captivating and soothing.
- **Emotional Regulation:** Provides a calming effect, helpful during moments of stress or overstimulation.
- **Fine Motor Skills:** Making and handling the bottle enhances dexterity.
- **Focus and Attention:** Watching the slow movement encourages mindfulness.
- **Creative Expression:** Personalizing the bottle allows for individual creativity.

Toys and Tools Used:

- **Clear Bottles:** Plastic preferred for safety.
- **Fillings:** Glitter, beads, sequins, food colouring.
- **Liquids:** Water, clear glue, baby oil.
- **Adhesives:** Strong glue to seal the cap.
- **Decorations:** Stickers or ribbons to personalize.

Consider creating themed bottles, such as an "Ocean Adventure" with blue water, fish-shaped confetti, and shells, or a "Space Explorer" bottle with black water, silver glitter, and star sequins. These themes can spark imagination and lead to storytelling or educational discussions about different subjects.

34. Sensory-Friendly Yoga

Introduce your child to the calming world of **Sensory-Friendly Yoga**, tailored to engage their senses gently while promoting physical well-being. Simple poses combined with mindful breathing can enhance body awareness and reduce anxiety.

How It's Done:

1. **Choose Simple Poses:** Select child-friendly poses like the butterfly, tree, cat-cow, and child's pose.
2. **Create a Calm Environment:** Use soft lighting, quiet music, or nature sounds to set a peaceful mood.
3. **Demonstrate the Poses:** Show each pose, guiding your child gently into position.
4. **Incorporate Breathing:** Teach deep breathing techniques, encouraging inhaling through the nose and exhaling through the mouth.
5. **Add Sensory Elements:** Use scented candles (out of reach), essential oils, or textured mats to enhance the sensory experience.

Benefits:

- **Physical Development:** Improves flexibility, strength, and coordination.
- **Emotional Regulation:** Promotes relaxation and reduces stress.
- **Body Awareness:** Enhances understanding of body position and movement.
- **Focus and Concentration:** Mindful practices improve attention span.
- **Sensory Integration:** Combines movement with tactile and olfactory stimuli.

Toys and Tools Used:

- **Yoga Mats:** Non-slip and comfortable.
- **Music or Sounds:** Soothing tunes or nature sounds.
- **Aromatherapy:** Essential oils like lavender or chamomile.
- **Visual Aids:** Picture cards showing poses.
- **Comfortable Clothing:** Allowing free movement.

To make yoga more engaging, weave stories into the session. For example, during the "Tree Pose," imagine being a tree swaying in the wind, or during "Cat-Cow," pretend to be animals on a farm. This imaginative approach can make the activity more relatable and fun.

35. Balloon Painting Adventure

Combine art and play with a **Balloon Painting Adventure**. Using balloons as painting tools introduces a unique texture and movement to the creative process, resulting in vibrant, unpredictable patterns and a whole lot of fun.

How It's Done:

1. **Prepare Balloons:** Inflate small balloons to a comfortable size for holding.
2. **Set Up the Painting Area:** Lay out large sheets of paper or canvas on the floor or a table covered with protective material.
3. **Choose Paints:** Use non-toxic, washable paints poured into shallow trays.
4. **Begin Painting:** Dip the balloons into the paint and press them onto the paper, experimenting with rolling, bouncing, or dragging them to create different effects.
5. **Explore and Create:** Encourage mixing colours and trying various movements to see how the patterns change.

Benefits:

- **Sensory Exploration:** The feel of the balloon and the movement required provide tactile and proprioceptive input.
- **Fine Motor Skills:** Gripping and manipulating the balloons enhance hand strength and coordination.
- **Creative Expression:** Offers a new medium to express artistic ideas.
- **Colour Mixing Understanding:** Observing how colours blend promotes learning about colour theory.
- **Emotional Joy:** The playful nature of the activity can elevate mood and reduce anxiety.

Toys and Tools Used:

- **Balloons:** Small to medium-sized, not overinflated.
- **Paints:** Washable and non-toxic varieties.
- **Paper or Canvas:** Large enough to allow free expression.
- **Protective Coverings:** Drop cloths, aprons, or old clothing.
- **Cleaning Supplies:** Warm water, soap, and towels for easy cleanup.

To add an element of surprise, you can fill some balloons with paint and let them pop over the canvas (with appropriate safety measures in place). This can create exciting splatter patterns and add to the sensory experience with unexpected sounds and visuals.

36. Sensory Pathway Walk

Design a **Sensory Pathway** in your home or yard where your child can walk, jump, and balance through different sensory stations. Each part of the path offers unique textures and activities, making movement fun and stimulating.

How It's Done:

1. **Plan the Pathway:** Decide on a route and what sensory experiences to include at each point.
2. **Create Stations:** Examples include:
   o **Texture Walk:** Stepping stones made of bubble wrap, foam mats, or carpet squares.
   o **Balance Beam:** A taped line or a low wooden beam to walk across.
   o **Jumping Pads:** Spots to hop from one to another.
   o **Wall Activities:** Places to press against handprints or stretch.
3. **Decorate the Path:** Use colourful tape, chalk, or signs to guide the way.
4. **Guide Your Child:** Walk through the pathway together, demonstrating each activity.
5. **Encourage Repetition:** Let your child explore the path at their own pace, repeating as desired.

Benefits:

- **Gross Motor Skills:** Improves balance, coordination, and spatial awareness.
- **Sensory Integration:** Combines tactile, proprioceptive, and vestibular input.
- **Physical Exercise:** Promotes healthy movement and energy release.
- **Following Directions:** Enhances understanding of sequences and instructions.

- **Creativity and Fun:** Allows for imaginative play as they navigate the path.

Toys and Tools Used:

- **Materials for Stations:** Bubble wrap, foam tiles, tape, chalk.
- **Decorations:** Stickers, signs, colourful markers.
- **Space:** An open area indoors or a safe outdoor space.

Consider incorporating themes like a jungle adventure, space journey, or superhero training course to make the pathway more engaging. You can also change the stations regularly to keep the experience fresh and challenging.

37. Sensory Story Stones

Craft **Sensory Story Stones** by painting or drawing images on smooth pebbles, then use them to inspire storytelling and imaginative play. This tactile and visual activity encourages language development and creativity.

How It's Done:

1. **Collect Smooth Stones:** Gather or purchase flat, smooth pebbles.
2. **Decorate the Stones:** Paint or draw simple images like animals, weather symbols, emotions, or objects.
3. **Dry and Seal:** Allow the artwork to dry and consider sealing with a clear varnish for durability.
4. **Storytelling Time:** Encourage your child to pick stones and create a story based on the images.
5. **Interactive Play:** Use the stones as props in playsets or sandbox adventures.

Benefits:

- **Language Skills:** Enhances vocabulary and narrative abilities.
- **Imagination Stimulation:** Sparks creative thinking and storytelling.
- **Fine Motor Skills:** Drawing or painting on stones improves dexterity.
- **Emotional Expression:** Allows exploration of feelings through characters and scenarios.

- **Sensory Engagement:** The feel of the stones provides tactile input.

Toys and Tools Used:

- **Stones:** Smooth, flat pebbles.
- **Art Supplies:** Acrylic paints, permanent markers.
- **Sealant (Optional):** Clear varnish or mod podge.
- **Storage Bag:** A pouch or box to keep the stones together.

You can tailor the stones to your child's interests, whether it's dinosaurs, fairy tales, or vehicles. Additionally, incorporating sensory elements like textured paints or adding glitter can enhance the tactile and visual appeal.

38. Cloud Dough Play

Discover the soft and moldable world of **Cloud Dough**, a sensory material that's easy to make and delightful to play with. It's softer than play dough and crumbles like sand but can be pressed together to form shapes.

How It's Done:

1. **Make the Cloud Dough:** Mix 8 parts flour with 1 part vegetable oil in a large bowl until it reaches a crumbly yet moldable consistency.
2. **Add Colours or Scents (Optional):** Use food colouring or essential oils to enhance the sensory experience.
3. **Set Up a Play Area:** Pour the cloud dough into a bin or tray.
4. **Provide Tools and Molds:** Include cups, cookie cutters, spoons, and small toys.
5. **Explore and Create:** Encourage your child to squeeze, mold, and let the dough crumble through their fingers.

Benefits:

- **Tactile Sensory Input:** The unique texture engages the sense of touch deeply.
- **Fine Motor Skills:** Manipulating the dough strengthens hand muscles.
- **Creative Play:** Building and shaping fosters imagination.

- **Calming Activity:** The repetitive motions can be soothing and stress-relieving.
- **Scientific Exploration:** Introduces concepts of mixtures and textures.

Toys and Tools Used:

- **Ingredients:** Flour, vegetable oil.
- **Mixing Bowl and Spoon:** For preparation.
- **Play Accessories:** Molds, scoops, figurines.
- **Protective Covering:** Tablecloth or mat for easy cleanup.

For an exciting twist, hide small treasures like plastic gems or toy dinosaurs in the cloud dough for your child to find. This adds an element of surprise and can keep them engaged longer. Remember to supervise play to prevent ingestion.

39. Homemade Musical Shakers

Craft **Homemade Musical Shakers** using everyday materials, and let your child explore rhythms and sounds. This activity combines creativity with auditory stimulation and can be a great introduction to music.

How It's Done:

1. **Gather Containers:** Use empty plastic bottles, film canisters, or small jars with secure lids.
2. **Select Fillings:** Choose items like rice, beans, beads, or small bells.
3. **Assemble the Shakers:** Fill the containers with the chosen materials, leaving some space for movement, and seal tightly.
4. **Decorate:** Let your child personalize the shakers with stickers, paint, or markers.
5. **Make Music:** Experiment with different shaking patterns, volumes, and rhythms.

Benefits:

- **Auditory Sensory Input:** Produces various sounds for exploration.
- **Fine Motor Skills:** Crafting and shaking enhance coordination.
- **Rhythm and Timing:** Introduces basic musical concepts.

- **Creative Expression:** Decorating allows artistic freedom.
- **Cause and Effect Learning:** Understanding how different fillings create different sounds.

Toys and Tools Used:

- **Containers:** Safe and sealable.
- **Fillings:** Rice, beans, beads.
- **Decorations:** Stickers, paints, ribbons.
- **Adhesive:** Glue or tape to secure lids.

Create shakers with different themes, like "Rainforest Sounds" using seeds and nuts or "Ocean Waves" with sand and small shells. Use the shakers to accompany songs, dances, or as part of a homemade band, encouraging social interaction and performance skills.

40. Bubble Wrap Roadway

Transform bubble wrap into an exciting **Bubble Wrap Roadway** for toy cars and feet alike. This activity combines auditory and tactile sensations as children drive, walk, or jump along the popping path.

How It's Done:

1. **Lay Out Bubble Wrap:** Spread bubble wrap sheets along the floor, securing them with tape if necessary.
2. **Create a Roadway:** Use markers or tape to draw lanes, stop signs, and other road elements on the bubble wrap.
3. **Provide Vehicles:** Supply toy cars, trucks, or trains.
4. **Play and Explore:** Encourage your child to drive the vehicles over the bubble wrap, listen to the pops, or walk and jump on it themselves.
5. **Incorporate Learning:** Introduce concepts like traffic rules, counting pops, or colour identification with traffic signs.

Benefits:

- **Sensory Stimulation:** Engages touch and hearing with the popping sensation.

- **Gross Motor Skills:** Movement improves coordination and balance.
- **Imaginative Play:** Setting up a roadway encourages storytelling and role-playing.
- **Fine Motor Skills:** Maneuvering vehicles enhances hand-eye coordination.
- **Cognitive Development:** Learning about traffic signs and rules introduces real-world concepts.

Toys and Tools Used:

- **Bubble Wrap:** Enough to create a pathway.
- **Toy Vehicles:** Cars, trucks, trains.
- **Markers or Tape:** For drawing on the bubble wrap.
- **Optional Props:** Toy traffic signs, buildings made from blocks.

Expand the roadway into a mini city by adding buildings constructed from boxes or blocks, creating bridges with cardboard, or setting up parking lots. Invite friends or siblings to join in, promoting social skills and cooperative play.

41. Sensory Water Play with Sponges

Dive into a refreshing experience with **Sensory Water Play with Sponges**. This activity involves using sponges of various shapes, sizes, and textures in water play, allowing children to explore different sensations while enhancing fine motor skills.

How It's Done:

1. **Gather Sponges:** Collect sponges of different textures—soft, coarse, natural sea sponges, or ones shaped like animals or objects.
2. **Prepare the Water Play Area:** Fill a shallow basin or tub with water. You can add a few drops of food colouring or non-toxic bubble bath for added sensory appeal.
3. **Introduce the Sponges:** Show your child how to dip the sponges in water, squeeze them to release the water, and feel the different textures.
4. **Explore Together:** Encourage your child to experiment with soaking, squeezing, and even transferring water from one container to another using the sponges.

5. **Add Accessories (Optional):** Include cups, funnels, or waterproof toys to extend the play.

Benefits:

- **Tactile Sensory Stimulation:** The feel of wet sponges provides rich tactile input.
- **Fine Motor Development:** Squeezing sponges strengthens hand and finger muscles.
- **Cause and Effect Understanding:** Observing how sponges absorb and release water teaches basic scientific concepts.
- **Calming Effect:** Water play can be soothing and help regulate emotions.
- **Creative Play:** Children can imagine washing toys, creating stories, or simply enjoy the sensory experience.

Toys and Tools Used:

- **Sponges:** Various types and textures.
- **Water Basin or Tub:** A safe container for water play.
- **Water:** Warm or cool, depending on preference.
- **Optional Accessories:** Cups, funnels, waterproof toys, food colouring.

For an added layer of fun, you can freeze water-soaked sponges overnight and let your child explore the cool sensations as they melt. This introduces temperature as another sensory element and can be especially enjoyable on a warm day.

42. Giant Drawing with Sidewalk Chalk

Unleash creativity outdoors with **Giant Drawing using Sidewalk Chalk**. This activity encourages children to use large motor movements to create big artwork on sidewalks or driveways, combining art with physical activity.

How It's Done:

1. **Get Sidewalk Chalk:** Choose brightly coloured, non-toxic chalk sticks that are easy to hold.

2. **Find a Safe Drawing Area:** A smooth, flat surface like a driveway, sidewalk, or patio is ideal.
3. **Encourage Big Movements:** Show your child how to make large strokes, draw big shapes, or even trace their own body outline.
4. **Create Together:** Draw alongside your child, perhaps collaborating on a giant mural or playing games like hopscotch.
5. **Incorporate Learning:** Use the opportunity to practice letters, numbers, shapes, or even write messages.

Benefits:

- **Gross Motor Skills:** Large movements enhance coordination and muscle development.
- **Creative Expression:** Offers a big canvas for imaginative artwork.
- **Sensory Stimulation:** The feel of chalk and the resistance against the pavement provide tactile feedback.
- **Visual-Motor Integration:** Combining visual input with motor actions improves these skills.
- **Outdoor Engagement:** Promotes fresh air and connection with the environment.

Toys and Tools Used:

- **Sidewalk Chalk:** Bright, chunky pieces suitable for small hands.
- **Safe Outdoor Space:** Ensure the area is free from traffic and hazards.
- **Protective Clothing:** Clothes that can get messy.
- **Optional Extras:** Spray bottles with water to create different effects.

You can turn this activity into an adventure by creating a "Chalk City" with roads, buildings, and parks drawn on the pavement. Children can use bicycles, scooters, or toy cars to navigate the city, adding layers of imaginative play and physical activity.

43. Fabric Sensory Bin

Introduce a variety of textures with a **Fabric Sensory Bin**, where children can explore different pieces of fabric, learning about textures, colours, and patterns through touch and visual stimulation.

How It's Done:

1. **Collect Fabric Pieces:** Gather scraps of fabric with diverse textures—silk, velvet, denim, fleece, lace, burlap, etc.
2. **Prepare the Bin:** Place all the fabric pieces into a large container or basket.
3. **Exploration Time:** Invite your child to feel each fabric, encouraging them to describe how it feels—soft, rough, smooth, scratchy.
4. **Sorting and Matching:** Create games like sorting fabrics by texture, colour, or pattern.
5. **Creative Uses:** Use the fabrics for pretend play, dress-up, or as props in storytelling.

Benefits:

- **Tactile Sensory Development:** Enhances the sense of touch through exposure to different textures.
- **Language Skills:** Expands vocabulary with descriptive words.
- **Cognitive Skills:** Sorting and categorizing promote critical thinking.
- **Imaginative Play:** Fabrics can become capes, blankets, or scenery in creative play.
- **Emotional Comfort:** Soft textures can provide a soothing sensory experience.

Toys and Tools Used:

- **Fabric Scraps:** Various textures, colours, and patterns.
- **Container:** A bin or basket to hold the fabrics.
- **Optional Items:** Scissors (with supervision) for cutting, glue for crafts.

You can extend this activity by incorporating a blindfolded "Guess the Fabric" game, where your child identifies fabrics by touch alone, enhancing their tactile discrimination skills.

44. Nature Sensory Collage

Combine art and nature with a **Nature Sensory Collage**. Collect natural items during a walk and use them to create a tactile and visual piece of art, fostering a connection with the environment.

How It's Done:

1. **Go on a Nature Walk:** Take a stroll in a park, garden, or around the neighborhood.
2. **Collect Items:** Gather leaves, flowers, twigs, grass, seeds, feathers—anything safe and interesting.
3. **Prepare the Base:** Use a large piece of cardboard or heavy paper as the collage base.
4. **Create the Collage:** Help your child arrange the items on the base and glue them down to create a unique artwork.
5. **Discuss Each Element:** Talk about where each item came from and its texture, colour, and scent.

Benefits:

- **Sensory Exploration:** Engages touch, sight, and smell through natural materials.
- **Fine Motor Skills:** Picking up and placing items enhances dexterity.
- **Environmental Awareness:** Encourages appreciation for nature.
- **Creative Expression:** Allows for individual artistic choices.
- **Language Development:** Discussing the items expands vocabulary.

Toys and Tools Used:

- **Natural Materials:** Collected during the walk.
- **Base Material:** Cardboard, poster board, or heavy paper.
- **Adhesive:** Glue sticks or liquid glue.
- **Optional Decorations:** Markers, paint, or stickers.

Consider framing the finished collage or displaying it prominently to celebrate your child's creation. This can boost their confidence and reinforce the value of their artistic efforts.

45. Scented Play Dough Creations

Enhance traditional play dough play by making **Scented Play Dough**, adding an olfactory dimension to the tactile experience. This activity stimulates multiple senses and can be tailored with different scents and colours.

How It's Done:

1. **Make Play Dough:** Use a simple homemade recipe or store-bought play dough.
2. **Add Scents:** Incorporate child-safe essential oils or food extracts like vanilla, lemon, peppermint, or cinnamon during the mixing process.
3. **Colour the Dough:** Use food colouring to match the scent (e.g., yellow for lemon, green for mint).
4. **Play Time:** Encourage your child to mold, shape, and create with the scented dough.
5. **Discuss the Scents:** Talk about the smells, perhaps relating them to foods or experiences.

Benefits:

- **Multi-Sensory Engagement:** Combines touch, smell, and sight.
- **Fine Motor Skills:** Molding and shaping improve hand strength.
- **Emotional Regulation:** The scents can have calming or invigorating effects.
- **Language Skills:** Describing scents enhances vocabulary.
- **Creative Expression:** Offers endless possibilities for imaginative creations.

Toys and Tools Used:

- **Play Dough Ingredients:** Flour, salt, water, oil, cream of tartar (for homemade version).
- **Scents:** Essential oils or food extracts.
- **Colouring:** Food colouring or natural dyes.
- **Play Accessories:** Rolling pins, cookie cutters, sculpting tools.

Be mindful of any scent sensitivities or allergies. You can also explore seasonal scents—for example, pumpkin spice in the fall or floral scents in the spring—to tie the activity to the time of year.

---

46. Mirror Tracing Activity

Challenge perception and coordination with a **Mirror Tracing Activity**. By placing a mirror next to a drawing surface, children attempt to trace or draw shapes while only looking at the reflection, enhancing spatial awareness and concentration.

How It's Done:

1. **Set Up the Mirror:** Place a small standing mirror perpendicular to a flat surface like a table.
2. **Prepare the Drawing Area:** Position a piece of paper next to the mirror.
3. **Choose Simple Shapes:** Start with basic shapes or letters drawn lightly on the paper.
4. **Explain the Task:** Instruct your child to trace over the shapes while only looking at the mirror image.
5. **Encourage Practice:** This task can be challenging; patience and encouragement are key.

Benefits:

- **Spatial Awareness:** Enhances understanding of spatial relationships.
- **Hand-Eye Coordination:** Improves fine motor control under novel conditions.
- **Concentration:** Requires focus and attention.
- **Problem-Solving Skills:** Engages the brain in adapting to a different perspective.
- **Fun Challenge:** Provides a unique and engaging activity.

Toys and Tools Used:

- **Mirror:** A small standing or handheld mirror.
- **Paper and Pencils:** For drawing and tracing.
- **Pre-drawn Shapes:** To trace over.

You can turn this into a game by timing how long it takes to complete a shape or by comparing attempts to see improvement. It's also interesting to let your child try drawing freehand while looking only at the mirror, encouraging creativity and laughter at the unexpected results.

47. Shadow Puppets Play

Ignite imagination with **Shadow Puppets Play**. Using hands or crafted puppets, children can create characters and stories projected onto a wall, combining visual and creative skills.

How It's Done:

1. **Set Up a Light Source:** Use a lamp or flashlight in a darkened room.
2. **Create a Screen:** A blank wall or a hanging white sheet works well.
3. **Demonstrate Hand Shadows:** Show how to make simple shapes like a bird or dog with your hands.
4. **Craft Puppets (Optional):** Cut out shapes from cardboard and attach them to sticks.
5. **Encourage Storytelling:** Let your child create scenes and narratives with the shadows.

Benefits:

- **Imaginative Play:** Fosters creativity and storytelling abilities.
- **Fine Motor Skills:** Manipulating hands or puppets enhances dexterity.
- **Visual Perception:** Understanding how shadows are formed and move.
- **Language Development:** Expands vocabulary and expressive language.
- **Emotional Expression:** Provides a medium to explore feelings through characters.

Toys and Tools Used:

- **Light Source:** Lamp, flashlight, or smartphone light.
- **Screen:** Blank wall or sheet.
- **Craft Materials:** Cardboard, scissors, sticks, tape for making puppets.

You can incorporate music or sound effects to enhance the performance. Recording the shadow play on video can also be a fun way to preserve the stories and watch them together later.

48. Sensory Obstacle Course

Set up a **Sensory Obstacle Course** indoors or outdoors that challenges your child's motor skills and engages their senses. Each station offers different activities like crawling under a blanket, walking on a textured path, or hopping over cushions.

How It's Done:

1. **Plan the Course:** Identify safe areas for each obstacle.
2. **Create Stations:**
   - **Crawl Tunnel:** Use a large cardboard box or drape a blanket over chairs.
   - **Texture Walk:** Lay out different textured mats or rugs to walk over.
   - **Balance Beam:** Use a strip of tape on the floor or a low, wide board.
   - **Jumping Spots:** Place cushions or hula hoops to hop between.
   - **Sensory Stop:** Include a bin with objects to feel or find.
3. **Explain the Course:** Guide your child through each obstacle, demonstrating if necessary.
4. **Time the Course (Optional):** For added excitement, use a timer to see how fast they can complete it.
5. **Repeat and Modify:** Change the obstacles or order to keep it interesting.

Benefits:

- **Gross Motor Skills:** Enhances balance, coordination, and strength.
- **Sensory Integration:** Combines tactile, proprioceptive, and vestibular input.
- **Problem-Solving Skills:** Navigating obstacles requires planning.
- **Physical Activity:** Promotes exercise and energy expenditure.
- **Confidence Building:** Successfully completing the course boosts self-esteem.

Toys and Tools Used:

- **Household Items:** Blankets, cushions, boxes, chairs.
- **Play Equipment:** Hula hoops, mats, balance boards.
- **Sensory Materials:** Textured objects, sensory bins.
- **Space:** An area large enough to safely set up the course.

Involve your child in designing the course to give them ownership and encourage creativity. You can also theme the course—like a superhero training camp or a jungle adventure—to make it more engaging.

49. Sensory Rice Play

Create a **Sensory Rice Bin** where children can scoop, pour, and run their hands through colourful rice, providing a soothing tactile experience. Adding toys or themes can extend the play and learning opportunities.

How It's Done:

1. **Prepare the Coloured Rice (Optional):** Dye uncooked rice using food colouring and a small amount of vinegar; let it dry completely.
2. **Fill a Large Bin:** Place the rice into a plastic tub or container.
3. **Add Tools and Toys:** Include scoops, funnels, cups, spoons, and small toys like cars, animals, or letters.
4. **Encourage Exploration:** Let your child freely play, transferring rice between containers, burying and finding objects, or simply enjoying the sensation.
5. **Introduce Themes:** Create scenarios like a construction site, beach, or treasure hunt.

Benefits:

- **Tactile Sensory Input:** The feel of rice stimulates touch.
- **Fine Motor Skills:** Scooping and pouring enhance hand coordination.
- **Cognitive Development:** Concepts like volume, measurement, and cause and effect are explored.
- **Language Skills:** Discussing the activity expands vocabulary.
- **Emotional Regulation:** The repetitive motions can be calming.

Toys and Tools Used:

- **Uncooked Rice:** White or coloured.
- **Container:** A bin large enough for play.
- **Utensils:** Scoops, spoons, funnels.
- **Small Toys:** Depending on the theme.

To minimize mess, place a sheet under the play area or set up outside. After playtime, the rice can be stored in an airtight container for future use.

50. Emotions Matching Game

Help your child recognize and understand different feelings with an **Emotions Matching Game**. Using cards or pictures showing various facial expressions, children match identical emotions or connect scenarios to feelings.

How It's Done:

1. **Create or Obtain Emotion Cards:** Use drawings or photos depicting different emotions—happy, sad, angry, surprised, etc.
2. **Explain Each Emotion:** Discuss what each facial expression represents.
3. **Play Matching Games:**
   ○ **Memory Game:** Place cards face down and take turns flipping two at a time to find matches.
   ○ **Scenario Matching:** Read a situation and have your child select the emotion that fits.
4. **Role-Playing:** Act out emotions and guess each other's feelings.
5. **Discuss Personal Experiences:** Encourage sharing times when they've felt each emotion.

Benefits:

- **Emotional Intelligence:** Enhances recognition and understanding of feelings.
- **Social Skills:** Improves empathy and interpersonal connections.
- **Language Development:** Expands vocabulary related to emotions.
- **Memory Skills:** Matching games boost memory and concentration.
- **Self-Expression:** Provides a safe space to talk about their own emotions.

Toys and Tools Used:

- **Emotion Cards:** Homemade or purchased.
- **Scenarios:** Simple stories or situations.
- **Space for Play:** A table or floor area.

This activity can be adapted to different levels by increasing the complexity of emotions or scenarios. Incorporating favourite characters or using mirrors to observe their own expressions can make the activity more engaging.

51. DIY Sensory Calm Down Jars

Create soothing **DIY Sensory Calm Down Jars** that children can shake and watch as the contents settle, providing a visual and tactile way to manage emotions and reduce stress. These jars are filled with glitter, sequins, or small objects suspended in liquid, mesmerizing as they swirl and slowly drift to the bottom.

How It's Done:

1. **Gather Materials:** You'll need a clear plastic jar or bottle with a tight-fitting lid, warm water, clear glue or glitter glue, glitter, food colouring (optional), and superglue or hot glue to seal the lid.
2. **Mix the Ingredients:** In the jar, mix warm water with clear glue; the more glue you use, the slower the glitter will settle. Add glitter and a few drops of food colouring if desired.
3. **Seal the Jar:** Ensure the lid is securely fastened, using superglue or hot glue around the rim before closing to prevent leaks.
4. **Test and Enjoy:** Shake the jar vigorously and watch as the glitter swirls and slowly settles. Encourage your child to use the jar when they need a calming moment.

Benefits:

- **Emotional Regulation:** Watching the slow movement can help reduce anxiety and provide a focus point during moments of stress.
- **Visual Sensory Stimulation:** The colourful, swirling patterns engage visual senses.
- **Mindfulness Practice:** Encourages deep breathing and relaxation as they watch the glitter settle.
- **Fine Motor Skills:** Making the jar involves pouring and measuring.

Tools and Materials Used:

- **Clear Plastic Jar or Bottle:** To avoid breakage.
- **Clear Glue or Glitter Glue:** Adjust the amount for settling speed.

- **Glitter and Sequins:** Various colours and shapes.
- **Food Colouring (Optional):** For tinted water.
- **Glue for Sealing:** Superglue or hot glue.

You can customize the jars with themes, such as ocean blues with shell-shaped glitter or galaxy purples with star sequins. Personalizing the jar can make it more special to your child, increasing its effectiveness as a calming tool. Always supervise young children during use to ensure they do not attempt to open the jar.

52. Fingerprint Art Projects

Explore creativity with **Fingerprint Art Projects**, where children use their own fingerprints dipped in washable ink or paint to create pictures, patterns, or even stories on paper. This hands-on activity is both fun and a great way to develop fine motor skills.

How It's Done:

1. **Prepare Materials:** Set up a workspace with paper, washable ink pads or paints, and wipes for easy cleanup.
2. **Demonstrate Techniques:** Show your child how to press their fingertip onto the ink pad or paint and then onto the paper.
3. **Create Together:** Encourage them to make various prints—fingerprints, thumbprints—and turn them into animals, flowers, or abstract designs by adding details with markers or pens.
4. **Tell a Story:** Use the fingerprint characters to create a story, fostering language skills and imagination.

Benefits:

- **Fine Motor Development:** Pressing and placing fingerprints requires control and precision.
- **Sensory Engagement:** The tactile sensation of ink or paint on fingers.
- **Creativity and Imagination:** Turning simple prints into art stimulates creative thinking.
- **Language and Storytelling Skills:** Narrating the art enhances communication abilities.

- **Paper or Cardstock:** A sturdy surface for artwork.
- **Washable Ink Pads or Non-toxic Paints:** Safe for skin contact.
- **Markers and Pens:** For adding details to fingerprint shapes.
- **Wipes or Towels:** For cleaning fingers between colours or at the end.

Fingerprint art can be themed around holidays, seasons, or favorite stories. For instance, making fingerprint pumpkins in the fall or fingerprint snowmen in winter. This activity also makes for wonderful homemade cards or gifts for family members.

53. Nature Sensory Walk

Engage in a **Nature Sensory Walk**, an outdoor adventure focusing on using all five senses to explore and connect with the environment. It's a mindful activity that encourages observation and appreciation of nature's details.

How It's Done:

1. **Choose a Safe Path:** Select a park, trail, or even your backyard.
2. **Sensory Checklist:** Create a simple list of things to find or experience with each sense (e.g., something rough, a bird song, the scent of a flower).
3. **Explore Mindfully:** Walk slowly, encouraging your child to focus on one sense at a time. Pause to touch tree bark, listen to leaves rustling, or watch insects.
4. **Discuss Discoveries:** Talk about what you both notice, using descriptive language.
5. **Collect Nature Treasures (Optional):** Gather small items like leaves or stones to examine later or use in crafts.

Benefits:

- **Sensory Integration:** Engages all senses, enhancing sensory processing abilities.
- **Mindfulness and Relaxation:** Promotes calmness and reduces stress.
- **Physical Activity:** Encourages gentle exercise and coordination.

- **Environmental Awareness:** Fosters a connection with nature and understanding of the ecosystem.
- **Language Development:** Expands vocabulary through descriptive conversations.

Tools and Materials Used:

- **Comfortable Clothing and Shoes:** Appropriate for walking and weather conditions.
- **Sensory Checklist or Journal:** To note observations.
- **Bag or Basket (Optional):** For collecting natural items.
- **Magnifying Glass or Binoculars (Optional):** For a closer look at plants and wildlife.

You can turn the walk into a scavenger hunt by including specific items to find. Additionally, taking photos can help your child recall and share their experiences later, further enhancing language skills and memory.

54. Magnetic Fishing Game

Create an interactive **Magnetic Fishing Game** where children "catch" fish made from paper clips and paper or foam, using a homemade fishing rod with a magnet. This activity combines creativity, fine motor skills, and problem-solving.

How It's Done:

1. **Make the Fish:** Cut out fish shapes from coloured paper or craft foam. Attach a paper clip to each fish as the "mouth."
2. **Create the Fishing Rod:** Tie a piece of string to a stick or dowel, and attach a small magnet at the end of the string.
3. **Set Up the Pond:** Place the fish in a shallow container or on the floor.
4. **Start Fishing:** Show your child how to lower the magnet to pick up the fish by their paper clip mouths.
5. **Add Challenges (Optional):** Label fish with numbers or letters for educational reinforcement.

Benefits:

- **Fine Motor Skills:** Maneuvering the fishing rod enhances hand-eye coordination.
- **Problem-Solving:** Figuring out how to catch the fish engages cognitive skills.
- **Educational Opportunities:** Incorporate learning by adding numbers, letters, or colours to the fish.
- **Imaginative Play:** Encourages storytelling and role-playing as fishermen.

Tools and Materials Used:

- **Craft Foam or Paper:** For making fish.
- **Paper Clips:** Attached to fish.
- **Stick or Dowel:** For the fishing rod.
- **String and Magnet:** To complete the rod.
- **Decorations (Optional):** Markers, googly eyes for fish.

This game can be easily adapted for group play, promoting social skills and turn-taking. You can also create different sea creatures or themes, like catching alphabet letters or shapes, to tailor the activity to your child's interests and learning goals.

---

55. Sensory Balloon Squishies

Make **Sensory Balloon Squishies**, tactile stress balls filled with various materials like flour, rice, or play dough, providing different textures for squeezing and manipulating. These squishies are great for sensory input and can help with self-regulation.

How It's Done:

1. **Choose Fillings:** Decide on materials like flour, rice, cornstarch, sand, or play dough.
2. **Fill the Balloons:** Stretch the balloon's opening over a funnel and fill with the chosen material. Fill until it's comfortably full but not overstretched.
3. **Tie the Balloon:** Securely tie the end to prevent leakage.

4. **Decorate (Optional):** Draw faces or patterns on the balloons with permanent markers.
5. **Use for Play and Relaxation:** Encourage your child to squeeze and squish the balloons to explore the textures and for stress relief.

Benefits:

- **Tactile Sensory Input:** Different fillings provide varied tactile experiences.
- **Fine Motor Strengthening:** Squeezing improves hand and finger muscles.
- **Emotional Regulation:** Can serve as a calming tool during moments of anxiety.
- **Exploration of Textures:** Introduces concepts of soft, hard, grainy, etc.
- **Creative Expression:** Decorating the squishies adds a personal touch.

Tools and Materials Used:

- **Balloons:** Strong, quality balloons to prevent bursting.
- **Fillings:** Flour, rice, cornstarch, sand, play dough.
- **Funnel:** For easier filling.
- **Permanent Markers (Optional):** For decorating.

Always supervise this activity, especially with younger children, to prevent accidental ingestion of fillings or choking hazards. You can also explore adding scents using a few drops of essential oil to the fillings for an olfactory component.

56. Body Sock Movement

Introduce the **Body Sock**, a stretchy, lycra fabric pouch that children can climb into, providing deep pressure input and resistance as they move. This activity is excellent for proprioceptive feedback and can be both calming and energizing.

How It's Done:

1. **Obtain a Body Sock:** These can be purchased online or made by sewing stretchy fabric into a sack with an opening.

2. **Explain and Demonstrate:** Show your child how to safely get into the body sock, ensuring their face remains uncovered for breathing and visibility.
3. **Encourage Movement:** Suggest activities like stretching, pushing against the fabric, pretending to be different animals, or practicing yoga poses.
4. **Create Games:** Play "Simon Says" with movements inside the body sock or have them navigate obstacle courses.

Benefits:

- **Proprioceptive Input:** Deep pressure and resistance help with body awareness.
- **Calming Effect:** The snug pressure can be soothing for many children.
- **Gross Motor Skills:** Enhances coordination and muscle strength.
- **Imaginative Play:** Sparks creativity as children imagine themselves in various scenarios.

Tools and Materials Used:

- **Body Sock:** Purchased or homemade from stretchy fabric.
- **Safe Space:** An open area free from obstacles.
- **Supervision:** To ensure safety during movement.

The body sock can be a valuable tool for transitioning between activities or calming down before bedtime. Always ensure the child is comfortable and can easily exit the body sock when they wish.

57. Taste Testing Adventure

Embark on a **Taste Testing Adventure** by sampling foods with different flavors—sweet, salty, sour, bitter, and umami. This activity can help children become more comfortable with new foods and expand their palate.

How It's Done:

1. **Prepare a Variety of Foods:** Select safe, age-appropriate foods representing different tastes, such as:

- Sweet: Fruit slices, small pieces of chocolate.
- Salty: Crackers, pretzels.
- Sour: Lemon wedges, sour candies.
- Bitter: Dark leafy greens, unsweetened cocoa.
- Umami: Cheese, mild soy sauce on rice.

2. **Set Up the Tasting Station:** Arrange small portions on a plate or in separate bowls.
3. **Introduce Each Taste:** Explain the taste category and encourage your child to try each one.
4. **Discuss Reactions:** Talk about how each food tastes and feels, noting likes and dislikes without pressure.
5. **Make It Fun:** Incorporate games like blindfold tasting or rating each food on a fun scale.

Benefits:

- **Sensory Exploration:** Engages the sense of taste and smell.
- **Food Acceptance:** Gently introduces new foods, potentially reducing picky eating habits.
- **Language Development:** Expands vocabulary with descriptive words.
- **Critical Thinking:** Encourages expressing opinions and preferences.
- **Social Skills:** Practicing manners and conversational skills during the activity.

Tools and Materials Used:

- **Variety of Foods:** Representing different taste categories.
- **Plates or Bowls:** For organization.
- **Utensils and Napkins:** For hygiene.
- **Optional Blindfold:** To focus on taste without visual cues.

Be mindful of any food allergies or sensitivities. Make the experience pressure-free, emphasizing exploration over consumption. This activity can be repeated with different foods from various cultures to expand the experience.

58. Bean Bag Toss Game

Set up a **Bean Bag Toss Game** to enhance hand-eye coordination, motor skills, and provide proprioceptive input. This classic game can be easily adapted for indoor or outdoor play and can include educational elements.

How It's Done:

1. **Create or Obtain Bean Bags:** Use small cloth bags filled with beans or rice, or make your own by filling socks or fabric squares.
2. **Set Up Targets:** Use hula hoops, buckets, or draw targets on cardboard or the ground with chalk.
3. **Explain the Game:** Show your child how to toss the bean bags underhand toward the targets.
4. **Add Educational Elements:** Label targets with numbers, letters, or colours to incorporate learning.
5. **Play Together:** Take turns tossing and keep score if appropriate.

Benefits:

- **Gross Motor Skills:** Improves throwing mechanics and coordination.
- **Hand-Eye Coordination:** Enhances the ability to aim and hit targets.
- **Proprioceptive Feedback:** The weight of the bean bags provides sensory input.
- **Social Skills:** Turn-taking and following game rules.
- **Math and Literacy Skills:** If incorporating numbers or letters.

Tools and Materials Used:

- **Bean Bags:** Store-bought or homemade.
- **Targets:** Buckets, hoops, drawn targets.
- **Space:** An area suitable for tossing.
- **Optional Decorations:** To theme the game (e.g., pirate treasure toss).

Adjust the difficulty by changing the distance to the targets or the size of the targets. The game can be played solo or with multiple players, making it versatile for different settings.

59. Ice Painting Activity

Combine art and sensory play with **Ice Painting**, using frozen paint cubes to create colourful artwork. As the ice melts, vibrant colours spread across the paper, offering a unique painting experience.

How It's Done:

1. **Prepare the Paint Cubes:** Mix washable, non-toxic liquid paint or food colouring with water and pour into ice cube trays. Insert popsicle sticks or toothpicks as handles, then freeze.
2. **Set Up the Work Area:** Cover a table with protective material and provide thick paper or cardstock.
3. **Begin Painting:** Remove the paint cubes from the freezer and let your child use them to draw and paint as they melt.
4. **Explore Colour Mixing:** Encourage experimenting with overlapping colours to see how they blend.
5. **Discuss the Process:** Talk about how the ice melts and the sensory feelings of cold and wet.

Benefits:

- **Sensory Exploration:** Engages touch (cold temperature), sight (colours), and the concept of melting.
- **Fine Motor Skills:** Holding and moving the ice cubes improves dexterity.
- **Creative Expression:** Offers a new medium for artistic creation.
- **Scientific Understanding:** Introduces basic concepts of states of matter and temperature effects.

Tools and Materials Used:

- **Ice Cube Trays:** For freezing the paint.
- **Washable Paint or Food Colouring:** Mixed with water.
- **Popsicle Sticks or Toothpicks:** As handles.
- **Paper:** Thick paper that can handle moisture.
- **Protective Coverings:** To keep the area clean.

This activity is great for warm days but can be done indoors with proper preparation. You can also freeze different shapes using silicone molds to add variety. Always ensure that the paints used are safe for skin contact.

60. Bubble Snake Maker

Create a **Bubble Snake Maker** for an exciting outdoor activity that produces long chains of bubbles, delighting children with visual and tactile sensations. It's simple to make using household items.

How It's Done:

1. **Gather Materials:** You'll need an empty plastic bottle, a sock or piece of fabric, a rubber band, dish soap, and water.
2. **Assemble the Bubble Maker:**
   - Cut the bottom off the plastic bottle.
   - Stretch the sock or fabric over the open bottom and secure it with a rubber band.
3. **Prepare the Bubble Solution:** Mix dish soap with water in a shallow container.
4. **Create Bubble Snakes:**
   - Dip the fabric-covered end into the bubble solution.
   - Blow gently through the mouthpiece to produce a bubble snake.
5. **Add Food Colouring (Optional):** Apply a few drops of food colouring to the fabric for colourful bubbles (use with caution as it can stain).

Benefits:

- **Oral Motor Skills:** Blowing strengthens muscles used for speech.
- **Visual Sensory Input:** Watching the bubbles form and float.
- **Gross Motor Skills:** Chasing and popping bubbles encourages movement.
- **Scientific Exploration:** Understanding how bubbles form and the effects of airflow.
- **Fun Outdoor Play:** Encourages enjoyment of the outdoors.

Tools and Materials Used:

- **Plastic Bottle:** Any size.
- **Sock or Fabric Piece:** Clean and thin.
- **Rubber Band:** To secure the fabric.
- **Dish Soap and Water:** For bubble solution.
- **Shallow Container:** To hold the solution.
- **Food Colouring (Optional):** For coloured bubbles.

Ensure that children do not inhale through the bottle to avoid ingesting soap. This activity is best done outside or in an area where soap and bubbles won't cause slippery surfaces. You can turn it into a game by seeing who can make the longest bubble snake or by counting how long the bubble chain lasts before popping.

61. Nature Painting with Leaves and Flowers

Immerse your child in the beauty of nature with **Nature Painting using Leaves and Flowers**. This activity involves using leaves, flowers, and other natural items as brushes or stamps to create unique artwork. It's a wonderful way to explore textures, shapes, and colours while fostering a connection with the outdoors.

How It's Done:

1. **Collect Natural Materials:** Take a walk in your garden, park, or backyard with your child to gather a variety of leaves, flowers, twigs, and grasses. Ensure that the plants are safe to handle and not harmful or allergic.
2. **Set Up the Painting Area:** Lay out a large sheet of paper or canvas on a flat surface. Prepare washable, non-toxic paints in shallow dishes or palettes.
3. **Explore Painting Techniques:**
   - **Stamping:** Dip leaves or flowers into the paint and press them onto the paper to leave imprints.
   - **Brushing:** Use a leafy branch or a bundle of grass as a paintbrush to create strokes and patterns.
   - **Printing:** Place a leaf under the paper and rub over it with crayons or pencils to reveal its texture.
4. **Encourage Creativity:** Let your child experiment with different materials and colours. They can create abstract designs, patterns, or even representational art like trees and landscapes.
5. **Discuss the Artwork:** Talk about the different textures and shapes that each natural item creates. Ask your child how they feel about their creation and what they enjoyed the most.

Benefits:

- **Sensory Exploration:** Engages touch, sight, and even smell as children handle natural materials and paints.
- **Fine Motor Skills:** Manipulating small items and painting enhances hand-eye coordination and dexterity.
- **Connection with Nature:** Fosters appreciation and curiosity about the environment.
- **Creative Expression:** Encourages individuality and artistic experimentation.
- **Language Development:** Discussing the process and materials expands vocabulary and communication skills.

Toys and Tools Used:

- **Natural Materials:** Leaves, flowers, twigs, grasses.
- **Painting Supplies:** Washable, non-toxic paints, brushes (optional), palettes.
- **Paper or Canvas:** Large sheets to allow freedom of expression.
- **Protective Coverings:** Tablecloths, aprons, or old clothing to keep mess contained.
- **Water and Towels:** For cleaning hands and materials.

To extend the activity, you can introduce themes like creating seasonal artwork (e.g., using colourful autumn leaves) or exploring patterns in nature. This activity not only stimulates creativity but also provides an opportunity to teach children about different plant species and their roles in the ecosystem.

62. Bubble Wrap Printing

Transform ordinary bubble wrap into a fun and engaging art tool with **Bubble Wrap Printing**. This activity allows children to explore textures and patterns by using bubble wrap to create unique prints and designs on paper.

How It's Done:

1. **Prepare the Materials:** Cut bubble wrap into manageable pieces or shapes. You can even wrap it around rolling pins or cardboard tubes for different effects.

2. **Set Up the Workspace:** Lay out large sheets of paper on a flat surface. Pour washable, non-toxic paint into shallow trays or plates.
3. **Begin Printing:**
    ○ **Stamping:** Dip the bubble wrap into the paint and press it onto the paper to create dotted patterns.
    ○ **Rolling:** If using a rolling pin wrapped with bubble wrap, roll it through the paint and then across the paper.
    ○ **Layering Colours:** Use different colours and overlap prints for a vibrant, multi-layered effect.
4. **Encourage Experimentation:** Let your child explore various techniques, such as dragging the bubble wrap or twisting it to see how the patterns change.
5. **Discuss the Results:** Talk about the textures and patterns created. Ask your child what they notice and how different methods produce different effects.

Benefits:

- **Sensory Stimulation:** The feel of the bubble wrap and the act of printing engage tactile senses.
- **Fine Motor Skills:** Handling and manipulating the bubble wrap enhances coordination.
- **Creative Exploration:** Offers a new medium for artistic expression.
- **Understanding Cause and Effect:** Observing how different techniques alter the outcome.
- **Emotional Expression:** Art can be a therapeutic outlet for emotions.

Toys and Tools Used:

- **Bubble Wrap:** Various sizes and shapes.
- **Paints:** Washable and non-toxic varieties.
- **Paper:** Large sheets or canvases.
- **Rolling Pins or Tubes (Optional):** For rolling techniques.
- **Protective Materials:** Table coverings, aprons, or old clothes.
- **Cleaning Supplies:** Water, soap, and towels for easy clean-up.

You can incorporate this activity into themed projects, such as creating underwater scenes where the bubble patterns resemble bubbles in the ocean or abstract art pieces. It's also a great way to reuse packaging materials, teaching children about recycling and sustainability.

63. Sound Hunt Adventure

Embark on a **Sound Hunt Adventure**, where children use their listening skills to identify and locate various sounds in their environment. This activity heightens auditory awareness and can be both exciting and calming.

How It's Done:

1. **Prepare a Sound List:** Create a list of sounds commonly found in your surroundings, such as a barking dog, a ticking clock, birds chirping, water running, or leaves rustling.
2. **Explain the Activity:** Tell your child that you'll be going on a sound hunt to find and identify different sounds.
3. **Explore Indoors and Outdoors:** Walk around your home or neighborhood, pausing to listen carefully at different spots.
4. **Identify and Record Sounds:** When your child hears a sound from the list, discuss what it is and where it's coming from. You can check it off the list or use stickers as markers.
5. **Add Challenges (Optional):** Introduce new sounds to identify or have your child close their eyes to focus solely on listening.

Benefits:

- **Auditory Processing Skills:** Enhances the ability to recognize and differentiate sounds.
- **Mindfulness and Focus:** Encourages being present and attentive to the environment.
- **Language Development:** Expands vocabulary related to sounds and their sources.
- **Emotional Awareness:** Discussing how certain sounds make them feel.
- **Connection with Environment:** Builds awareness of the surrounding world.

Toys and Tools Used:

- **Sound List:** Written or visual aids, depending on the child's reading level.
- **Recording Device (Optional):** Use a phone or recorder to capture sounds and listen back later.
- **Notebook and Pen:** For older children to take notes or draw what they hear.

This activity can be adapted for different settings, such as a park, beach, or city environment, each offering unique sounds. It can also be a stepping stone to discussions about nature, weather, or urban life, depending on the sounds encountered.

64. Clay Modeling Creations

Unleash your child's imagination with **Clay Modeling Creations**. Using air-dry clay or modeling clay, children can sculpt, mold, and build anything they envision, from animals and figures to abstract forms.

How It's Done:

1. **Choose the Clay:** Select air-dry clay for creations that can harden and be kept, or modeling clay that remains flexible for continuous play.
2. **Set Up the Workspace:** Provide a clean, flat surface covered with wax paper or a plastic mat to prevent sticking.
3. **Provide Tools and Accessories:** Offer tools like plastic knives, rolling pins, cookie cutters, and stamps. Natural materials like sticks, leaves, and stones can also add interesting textures.
4. **Encourage Creativity:** Let your child decide what they'd like to make. Offer ideas if they need inspiration but allow them to lead.
5. **Decorate and Display:** If using air-dry clay, once it hardens, your child can paint their creations. Display their artwork proudly to boost confidence.

Benefits:

- **Fine Motor Skills:** Manipulating clay strengthens hand muscles and coordination.
- **Sensory Experience:** The texture of clay provides tactile stimulation.
- **Creative Expression:** Fosters imagination and problem-solving.
- **Emotional Outlet:** Art allows for the expression of feelings in a non-verbal way.
- **Patience and Focus:** The process encourages concentration and perseverance.

Toys and Tools Used:

- **Clay:** Air-dry or modeling clay in various colours.
- **Modeling Tools:** Rolling pins, cutters, stamps.
- **Natural Materials (Optional):** Leaves, twigs, stones for texture.
- **Protective Coverings:** Table mats or wax paper.
- **Paints and Brushes (Optional):** For decorating hardened creations.

Consider setting themes or challenges, like creating a favorite animal or building a miniature garden. Group activities can promote social skills, as children can collaborate on larger projects or share techniques.

65. Scarf Dancing

Get moving with **Scarf Dancing**, an activity that combines music, movement, and sensory play. Using lightweight scarves or pieces of fabric, children can dance, twirl, and explore rhythms, enhancing their physical coordination and expressiveness.

How It's Done:

1. **Select Music:** Choose a variety of songs with different tempos and moods.
2. **Provide Scarves:** Use chiffon scarves, bandanas, or any lightweight fabric that flows easily.
3. **Demonstrate Movements:** Show how to wave the scarves, make circles, toss them gently into the air, or wrap them around.
4. **Encourage Free Expression:** Let your child move to the music in any way they feel inspired, using the scarves to enhance their movements.
5. **Introduce Games (Optional):**
   - **Freeze Dance:** Pause the music and freeze in place.
   - **Mimic Movements:** Take turns leading and copying each other's actions.

Benefits:

- **Gross Motor Skills:** Enhances coordination, balance, and spatial awareness.
- **Sensory Stimulation:** The feel of the fabric and the visual of it moving through the air engage touch and sight.

- **Emotional Expression:** Music and movement allow children to express feelings.
- **Rhythm and Timing:** Dancing to music improves understanding of beats and rhythms.
- **Social Interaction:** If dancing with others, promotes cooperation and turn-taking.

Toys and Tools Used:

- **Scarves or Fabric Pieces:** Lightweight and safe for waving.
- **Music Player:** Device to play selected songs.
- **Open Space:** Area free from obstacles for safe movement.

Scarf dancing can be adapted for different themes, such as pretending to be butterflies, waves, or weather elements like wind and rain. It's a joyful way to incorporate physical activity into the day and can be especially beneficial for children who may be reluctant to engage in more structured exercises.

66. DIY Sensory Bag Exploration

Create **DIY Sensory Bags** filled with various materials for squishing, pressing, and exploring without the mess. These sealed bags provide a safe way for children to experience different textures and visual effects, making them ideal for tactile and visual stimulation.

How It's Done:

1. **Gather Materials:** You'll need sturdy, sealable plastic bags (like freezer bags), duct tape, and filling materials such as hair gel, water beads, glitter, small toys, or coloured water.
2. **Prepare the Bags:**
   - Fill the bag with the chosen materials, leaving some space to allow movement.
   - Press out excess air before sealing tightly.
   - Reinforce the edges and seal with duct tape to prevent leaks.
3. **Explore Sensory Play:** Place the bag on a flat surface and encourage your child to press, squeeze, and manipulate the contents.

4. **Incorporate Learning Elements:** Add letters, numbers, or shapes inside the bag for educational interaction.
5. **Supervise Play:** Ensure the bag remains sealed during use.

Benefits:

- **Tactile Sensory Input:** Provides touch sensations without direct contact with potentially messy materials.
- **Fine Motor Skills:** Manipulating the bag enhances hand strength and coordination.
- **Visual Engagement:** Glitter and colourful items capture visual interest.
- **Emotional Regulation:** The repetitive motions can be calming and soothing.
- **Safe Exploration:** Ideal for children who may have aversions to touching certain textures directly.

Toys and Tools Used:

- **Plastic Sealable Bags:** Heavy-duty to withstand pressure.
- **Fillings:** Hair gel, glitter, beads, small toys, water beads, coloured water.
- **Duct Tape:** For sealing and reinforcing.
- **Flat Surface:** Table or floor area for play.

You can theme the sensory bags according to seasons or holidays, such as orange gel with leaf confetti for autumn or clear gel with snowflake sequins for winter. Always supervise the use of sensory bags to ensure safety.

67. Footprint Trail

Create a **Footprint Trail** by painting the soles of your child's feet and letting them walk across a large sheet of paper or canvas. This activity combines sensory play with gross motor skills and results in a unique piece of art.

How It's Done:

1. **Prepare the Area:** Lay out a long sheet of butcher paper or old wallpaper on a flat surface, preferably outdoors or in a space that can get messy.

2. **Choose Safe Paints:** Use washable, non-toxic paints suitable for skin contact.
3. **Paint the Feet:** Apply a layer of paint to the soles of your child's feet using a brush or sponge.
4. **Create the Trail:** Have your child walk, dance, or hop along the paper, leaving colourful footprints behind.
5. **Explore Patterns:** Encourage different movements, like tiptoeing or jumping, to see how the prints change.

Benefits:

- **Sensory Stimulation:** The feeling of paint on feet and the texture underfoot engage tactile senses.
- **Gross Motor Development:** Walking and balancing enhance coordination.
- **Creative Expression:** Results in a personalized artwork.
- **Body Awareness:** Helps children understand movement and the effects of their actions.
- **Fun Physical Activity:** Promotes enjoyment of movement and exercise.

Toys and Tools Used:

- **Large Paper or Canvas:** Long enough to allow movement.
- **Washable Paints:** Non-toxic and safe for skin.
- **Brushes or Sponges:** For applying paint.
- **Water and Towels:** For cleaning feet after the activity.
- **Protective Coverings:** To protect surrounding areas.

Consider using multiple colours or even glitter paint for added excitement. The finished footprint trail can be displayed as a fun reminder of the activity or cut into sections for keepsakes. Always ensure safety by preventing slipping; you may place the paper over a non-slip mat or secure it to the ground.

68. Storytelling with Puppets

Encourage language skills and creativity through **Storytelling with Puppets**. Using hand puppets, finger puppets, or even sock puppets, children can act out stories, express emotions, and explore different characters.

How It's Done:

1. **Provide Puppets:** Use store-bought puppets or create your own using socks, paper bags, or felt.
2. **Set the Stage:** Create a simple puppet theater using a cardboard box or a curtain hung in a doorway.
3. **Develop a Story:** Encourage your child to come up with a storyline or provide a familiar tale to enact.
4. **Perform Together:** Take turns being different characters, or have your child perform for family members.
5. **Discuss the Story:** After the performance, talk about the plot, characters, and any lessons learned.

Benefits:

- **Language Development:** Enhances vocabulary, sentence structure, and storytelling abilities.
- **Emotional Expression:** Allows children to explore feelings through characters.
- **Social Skills:** Promotes turn-taking, listening, and cooperation.
- **Imagination and Creativity:** Encourages original ideas and creative thinking.
- **Confidence Building:** Performing can boost self-esteem.

Toys and Tools Used:

- **Puppets:** Hand, finger, or sock puppets.
- **Puppet Theater (Optional):** A simple setup for performances.
- **Craft Supplies (Optional):** For making puppets—socks, googly eyes, glue, felt, markers.
- **Audience Members:** Family or friends to watch and engage.

This activity can be adapted for solo play or group settings. You can introduce themes, such as adventures, problem-solving scenarios, or educational topics, to align with learning objectives or interests.

---

69. Sensory Exploration with Feathers

Use **Feather Sensory Exploration** to engage your child's sense of touch and movement. Feathers offer a soft, delicate texture that's intriguing to explore, and they can be used in various playful activities.

How It's Done:

1. **Gather Feathers:** Use craft feathers available at art supply stores. Ensure they are clean and safe for handling.
2. **Set Up the Activity:** Spread the feathers on a clean surface or place them in a shallow container.
3. **Explore Tactile Sensations:** Encourage your child to touch, stroke, and rub the feathers on their hands, arms, or cheeks.
4. **Incorporate Movement Games:**
   - **Feather Blowing:** Use straws or breath to blow feathers across a table.
   - **Feather Drop:** Stand on a chair and let feathers drift down, watching their movement.
   - **Balance Challenge:** Try to balance a feather on different body parts.
5. **Art Projects (Optional):** Use feathers to create collages or add to drawings.

Benefits:

- **Tactile Sensory Input:** Soft textures stimulate the sense of touch.
- **Fine Motor Skills:** Picking up and manipulating feathers enhances dexterity.
- **Oral Motor Skills:** Blowing feathers helps strengthen muscles used for speech.
- **Visual Tracking:** Watching feathers float improves eye movement control.
- **Mindfulness and Relaxation:** The gentle nature of feathers can be calming.

Toys and Tools Used:

- **Feathers:** Clean craft feathers in various colours.
- **Straws (Optional):** For blowing games.
- **Art Supplies (Optional):** Glue, paper, markers for crafting.

Always supervise feather activities to prevent ingestion or inhalation, especially with younger children. You can also use this opportunity to discuss birds, habitats, and the function of feathers, integrating educational content into the play.

---

70. DIY Wind Chimes

Craft **DIY Wind Chimes** using simple materials to create beautiful sounds when the wind blows. This activity combines creativity, fine motor skills, and an introduction to music and environmental science.

How It's Done:

1. **Gather Materials:** You'll need items like sticks, shells, beads, bells, metal washers, keys, or bamboo pieces, along with string or fishing line.
2. **Create the Base:** Use a sturdy stick or a metal hoop as the top of the wind chime.
3. **Assemble the Chimes:**
   o Tie strings of varying lengths to the base.
   o Attach different objects to the ends of the strings, ensuring they can move freely and touch each other to produce sounds.
4. **Decorate (Optional):** Paint or embellish the base and chime pieces.
5. **Hang Your Wind Chime:** Place it outside where it can catch the wind, such as on a porch or near a window.

Benefits:

- **Fine Motor Skills:** Threading and tying enhance coordination.
- **Auditory Sensory Input:** Produces soothing sounds that engage hearing.
- **Creative Expression:** Personalizing the wind chime fosters creativity.
- **Understanding Cause and Effect:** Observing how wind movement creates sound.
- **Environmental Awareness:** Introduces concepts of weather and natural elements.

Toys and Tools Used:

- **Base Material:** Stick, hoop, or wooden dowel.
- **Chime Pieces:** Shells, beads, bells, metal objects.
- **String or Fishing Line:** For assembly.
- **Decorations (Optional):** Paints, ribbons, feathers.
- **Tools:** Scissors, possibly a drill for making holes.

This project can be adapted to focus on recycling by using found objects like old keys or broken jewelry. It's also an opportunity to discuss the science of sound, vibrations, and how different materials produce different tones.

71. Sponge Painting Extravaganza

Unleash your child's creativity with a **Sponge Painting Extravaganza**. This activity involves using sponges of various shapes and textures to apply paint to paper, creating unique patterns and designs. It's a delightful way for children to explore colours, textures, and artistic expression while engaging their senses.

How It's Done:

1. **Gather Materials:**
   - Collect sponges of different sizes and textures. You can use kitchen sponges, bath sponges, or craft sponges cut into various shapes like circles, squares, stars, or hearts.
   - Prepare washable, non-toxic paints in a palette or shallow containers.
   - Lay out large sheets of paper or canvas on a flat surface covered with a protective cloth or newspapers.
2. **Set Up the Painting Area:**
   - Arrange the sponges and paints within easy reach.
   - Provide aprons or old clothing to keep your child clean.
3. **Demonstrate Techniques:**
   - Show your child how to dip a sponge into the paint and press it onto the paper to make a print.
   - Encourage experimenting with different amounts of paint and pressure to see how the prints change.
4. **Encourage Creative Exploration:**
   - Let your child choose colours and sponge shapes freely.
   - Suggest creating patterns, abstract designs, or even forming images like flowers, animals, or landscapes.
   - Allow them to mix colours on the sponge or the paper to discover new hues.

5. **Discuss the Artwork:**
   - o Talk about the colours used and the patterns created.
   - o Ask open-ended questions like, "What do you like about this shape?" or "How does this colour make you feel?"

Benefits:

- **Sensory Stimulation:** The texture of the sponges and the feel of paint engage the tactile senses.
- **Fine Motor Skills:** Grasping sponges and applying paint enhances hand-eye coordination and muscle control.
- **Colour Recognition and Mixing:** Experimenting with colours helps children learn about primary and secondary colours.
- **Creative Expression:** Provides an open-ended platform for artistic expression and imagination.
- **Emotional Outlet:** Art can be therapeutic, allowing children to express feelings non-verbally.

Toys and Tools Used:

- **Sponges:** Various sizes and shapes, store-bought or homemade.
- **Paints:** Washable, non-toxic finger paints or tempera paints.
- **Paper or Canvas:** Large sheets to accommodate big designs.
- **Protective Materials:** Table coverings, aprons, old clothes.
- **Water and Towels:** For rinsing sponges and cleaning up.

To add variety, consider incorporating other materials like bubble wrap or textured fabrics for printing alongside the sponges. You can also theme the activity around seasons or holidays, using appropriate colours and shapes (e.g., orange and black sponges cut into pumpkin and bat shapes for Halloween). This activity not only fosters creativity but also provides a fun, hands-on learning experience that can be enjoyed by children of various ages and abilities.

72. Sensory Yoga Adventure

Introduce your child to a **Sensory Yoga Adventure**, combining simple yoga poses with sensory elements like sounds, scents, and tactile objects. This activity promotes physical well-being, mindfulness, and sensory integration in a playful and engaging manner.

How It's Done:

1. **Create a Calm Environment:**
   - Choose a quiet space free from distractions.
   - Play soft background music or nature sounds.
   - Dim the lights or use natural lighting.
2. **Incorporate Sensory Elements:**
   - **Scents:** Use a diffuser with child-safe essential oils like lavender or chamomile.
   - **Textures:** Provide a soft yoga mat, plush rug, or tactile cushions.
   - **Visuals:** Place calming images or use a projector to display nature scenes.
3. **Select Simple Poses:**
   - Introduce basic yoga poses suitable for children, such as:
     - **Tree Pose:** Balancing on one foot with arms raised.
     - **Cat-Cow Pose:** Arching and rounding the back on all fours.
     - **Butterfly Pose:** Sitting with the soles of the feet together.
     - **Downward-Facing Dog:** Forming an inverted V-shape with the body.
4. **Guide the Yoga Session:**
   - Use imaginative storytelling to make poses engaging:
     - "Let's become tall trees swaying in the wind."
     - "Imagine you're a cat stretching after a nap."
   - Encourage deep breathing by inhaling through the nose and exhaling through the mouth.
5. **End with Relaxation:**
   - Conclude the session with a resting pose (savasana), lying down quietly.
   - Offer a gentle forehead massage or place a cool, damp cloth over their eyes (if they are comfortable).

Benefits:

- **Physical Development:** Enhances flexibility, strength, balance, and coordination.
- **Sensory Integration:** Combines movement with sensory stimuli for holistic engagement.
- **Emotional Regulation:** Promotes relaxation, reduces anxiety, and improves mood.

- **Mindfulness and Focus:** Encourages present-moment awareness and concentration.
- **Imaginative Play:** Storytelling elements make yoga fun and accessible.

Toys and Tools Used:

- **Yoga Mat or Soft Surface:** For comfort during poses.
- **Music or Sounds:** Gentle tunes or nature recordings.
- **Aromatherapy Diffuser (Optional):** With child-safe essential oils.
- **Visual Aids:** Posters or cards illustrating poses.
- **Comfort Items:** Cushions, blankets, or stuffed animals.

Sensory yoga can be adapted to suit individual needs and preferences. For children who may be sensitive to certain stimuli, customize the sensory elements accordingly. Incorporating themes like "jungle adventure" or "ocean exploration" can further enhance engagement. Practicing yoga together also provides an opportunity for bonding and promoting a healthy, active lifestyle.

73. Interactive Storytime with Props

Elevate reading sessions by engaging in **Interactive Storytime with Props**. This activity involves using tactile objects, costumes, or puppets related to the story to make reading more dynamic and immersive. It's an excellent way to enhance comprehension, vocabulary, and enjoyment of books.

How It's Done:

1. **Select an Appropriate Book:**
   - Choose a story with vivid imagery and opportunities for interaction, such as fairy tales, adventure stories, or books with repetitive phrases.
2. **Gather Props and Costumes:**
   - Collect items that represent characters or elements from the story. For example:
     - Animal puppets or stuffed toys.
     - Hats, scarves, or simple costume pieces.
     - Objects like a toy boat, magic wand, or faux food items.
3. **Prepare the Reading Space:**

- Set up a comfortable area with cushions and good lighting.
- Arrange the props within easy reach.

4. **Engage in the Story:**
   - As you read, encourage your child to participate by:
     - Holding or manipulating props that correspond to the narrative.
     - Acting out scenes or mimicking character actions.
     - Making sound effects or repeating catchphrases.

5. **Ask Open-Ended Questions:**
   - Discuss the story by asking questions like:
     - "What do you think will happen next?"
     - "How do you think the character feels?"
     - "What would you do in that situation?"

Benefits:

- **Enhanced Comprehension:** Interactive elements help children understand and remember the story.
- **Language Development:** Expands vocabulary and encourages expressive language.
- **Social and Emotional Skills:** Exploring characters' feelings promotes empathy.
- **Imagination Stimulation:** Brings the story to life, fostering creativity.
- **Attention and Focus:** Keeps children engaged and attentive during reading.

Toys and Tools Used:

- **Books:** With engaging stories suitable for your child's age.
- **Props and Costumes:** Related to the story's characters and events.
- **Comfortable Seating:** Cushions, blankets, or a cozy reading nook.
- **Optional Sound Effects:** Instruments or recordings to enhance the atmosphere.

You can extend this activity by creating simple crafts related to the story before or after reading, such as making a paper crown for a princess tale or constructing a cardboard spaceship for a space adventure. Recording your interactive story sessions can also be a delightful way to preserve memories and encourage your child to see their progress over time.

74. Sensory Foot Spa

Pamper your child with a relaxing **Sensory Foot Spa** experience. Soaking feet in warm water with added textures and scents can be both calming and stimulating, providing tactile and olfactory sensory input.

How It's Done:

1. **Prepare the Foot Spa:**
   - Fill a shallow basin or tub with warm (not hot) water.
   - Add Epsom salts, mild bubble bath, or essential oils like lavender or chamomile for a soothing scent.
2. **Introduce Textures:**
   - Include smooth pebbles, marbles, or water beads at the bottom of the basin for tactile stimulation.
   - Ensure all items are safe and large enough to prevent choking hazards.
3. **Set the Mood:**
   - Dim the lights or use soft lighting.
   - Play gentle background music or nature sounds.
4. **Guide the Experience:**
   - Encourage your child to swirl their feet, feel the textures underfoot, and enjoy the warmth.
   - Offer a gentle foot massage if they are comfortable with touch.
5. **Extend the Activity:**
   - Provide a soft towel for drying and perhaps follow up with moisturizing lotion.
   - Discuss how the experience felt, using descriptive words to enhance vocabulary.

Benefits:

- **Tactile Sensory Input:** The combination of warm water and textures engages the sense of touch.
- **Relaxation and Stress Relief:** Can reduce anxiety and promote calmness.
- **Body Awareness:** Helps children become more attuned to their bodies and sensations.
- **Language Development:** Describing the experience enhances expressive language.
- **Emotional Connection:** Provides an opportunity for bonding and trust-building.

Toys and Tools Used:

- **Basin or Tub:** Large enough for comfortable foot placement.
- **Additives:** Epsom salts, mild bubble bath, essential oils.
- **Textures:** Smooth pebbles, marbles, water beads.
- **Towels and Lotion:** For drying and post-soak care.
- **Music or Sounds:** To create a serene environment.

Always supervise this activity to ensure safety, especially with younger children. Customize the sensory elements based on your child's preferences; some may enjoy cooler water or different scents. This activity can also be adapted into a full "spa day" with hand soaks, face masks (using gentle, child-safe products), or nail painting for added fun.

75. Sensory Play with Kinetic Sand

Delve into the fascinating world of **Kinetic Sand,** a moldable, tactile material that flows through fingers like slow-moving liquid but can be shaped and sculpted like wet sand. It's an excellent medium for sensory play, creativity, and fine motor skill development.

How It's Done:

1. **Acquire Kinetic Sand:**
   - Purchase commercially available kinetic sand or make your own using sand and cornstarch with a bit of oil.
2. **Set Up the Play Area:**
   - Place the sand in a large, shallow container or sensory table.
   - Lay down a protective mat or cloth to catch any spills.
3. **Provide Tools and Molds:**
   - Include items like sandcastle molds, cookie cutters, small cups, spoons, and plastic knives.
   - Offer figurines or toys for imaginative play scenarios.
4. **Encourage Exploration:**
   - Let your child feel the sand, noticing its unique texture.
   - Demonstrate how to pack it into molds or build structures.
   - Encourage creativity by making shapes, letters, or scenes.
5. **Discuss the Experience:**

- o Talk about how the sand feels and moves.
- o Ask questions like, "What are you making?" or "How does it feel when it flows through your fingers?"

Benefits:

- **Tactile Sensory Stimulation:** Engages the sense of touch with a unique texture.
- **Fine Motor Skills:** Manipulating the sand enhances hand strength and coordination.
- **Creative Expression:** Offers endless possibilities for building and sculpting.
- **Emotional Regulation:** The repetitive motions can be soothing and stress-relieving.
- **Cognitive Development:** Concepts like cause and effect, volume, and structure are explored.

Toys and Tools Used:

- **Kinetic Sand:** Commercial or homemade.
- **Container:** Large tray or bin for play.
- **Tools and Molds:** Variety of shapes and utensils.
- **Protective Coverings:** To keep the play area clean.
- **Cleaning Supplies:** For easy cleanup afterward.

Kinetic sand is less messy than traditional sand and sticks to itself, making it easier to clean up. However, it's still advisable to supervise play to prevent ingestion and to ensure that the sand stays within the play area. This activity can be themed around holidays, seasons, or interests, such as building a snowy landscape in winter or a desert scene with toy animals.

76. Music and Movement Freeze Dance

Combine physical activity with auditory stimulation in a lively game of **Music and Movement Freeze Dance**. Children dance to upbeat music and must freeze in place when the music stops, enhancing their listening skills, coordination, and self-control.

How It's Done:

1. **Select Music:**
   - Choose energetic songs that your child enjoys.
   - Mix different genres to expose them to various rhythms and beats.
2. **Explain the Game Rules:**
   - When the music plays, everyone dances freely.
   - When the music stops, everyone must freeze in their current position.
   - Anyone who moves while frozen is playfully reminded to stay still until the music resumes.
3. **Begin the Game:**
   - Start the music and let your child dance.
   - Pause the music at random intervals to keep the game unpredictable.
   - Join in the fun to encourage participation.
4. **Add Challenges (Optional):**
   - Incorporate specific dance moves or poses.
   - Use props like scarves or ribbons to enhance movement.
   - Adjust the length of music and pause times to increase difficulty.
5. **Conclude with Cool-Down:**
   - End the session with a slower song and gentle movements to relax.

Benefits:

- **Gross Motor Skills:** Dancing improves coordination, balance, and muscle strength.
- **Auditory Processing:** Listening for music cues enhances attention and response to sounds.
- **Self-Regulation:** Learning to control movement and impulses during the "freeze" moments.
- **Social Interaction:** Encourages turn-taking and following group rules.
- **Emotional Expression:** Provides an outlet for energy and emotions through movement.

Toys and Tools Used:

- **Music Player:** Device to play and pause songs.
- **Playlist:** A selection of appropriate and enjoyable music.
- **Open Space:** Safe area for dancing without obstacles.
- **Props (Optional):** Scarves, ribbons, or musical instruments.

This activity is easily adaptable for different ages and abilities. For children who may be less mobile, movements can be modified to clapping hands or nodding heads. Freeze dance can also be themed around animals, emotions, or actions, where children freeze in specific poses (e.g., like a statue, tree, or favorite character).

77. Bubble Science Experiment

Combine fun and learning with a **Bubble Science Experiment**. Children can explore the properties of bubbles by making their own bubble solution, creating bubble wands, and observing how bubbles form and behave.

How It's Done:

1. **Prepare the Bubble Solution:**
   - Mix 4 cups of warm water with 1/2 cup of dish soap and 1/4 cup of glycerin or corn syrup to strengthen the bubbles.
   - Stir gently to avoid creating foam.
2. **Create Bubble Wands:**
   - Use pipe cleaners, straws, or wire to form different shapes like circles, squares, or triangles.
   - Encourage creativity in designing unique wands.
3. **Conduct Experiments:**
   - Test which wand shapes produce the best bubbles.
   - Observe the colours in bubbles when sunlight passes through them.
   - Try blowing bubbles in different weather conditions (e.g., humid vs. dry days).
4. **Ask Scientific Questions:**
   - "What happens if we blow gently versus forcefully?"
   - "How do bubbles stick together?"
   - "Why do bubbles pop?"
5. **Record Observations:**
   - Draw pictures or write notes about the experiments.
   - Take photos to document different bubble sizes and shapes.

Benefits:

- **Scientific Exploration:** Introduces basic concepts of chemistry and physics.

- **Fine Motor Skills:** Manipulating wands and blowing bubbles enhances coordination.
- **Curiosity and Inquiry:** Encourages asking questions and seeking answers.
- **Sensory Engagement:** Visual and tactile stimuli from bubbles.
- **Joyful Play:** Bubbles often bring excitement and laughter.

Toys and Tools Used:

- **Bubble Solution Ingredients:** Water, dish soap, glycerin or corn syrup.
- **Containers:** For mixing and holding the solution.
- **Materials for Wands:** Pipe cleaners, straws, wire, or cookie cutters.
- **Notebook and Pen (Optional):** For recording observations.
- **Protective Clothing (Optional):** To stay clean during play.

This activity can be extended by exploring bubble art, where children blow bubbles onto paper to create colourful patterns. Additionally, discussing the science behind bubbles' spherical shape and surface tension can enrich the educational aspect. Always supervise young children to ensure they do not ingest the bubble solution.

78. Mirror Play and Facial Expressions

Engage in **Mirror Play** to help children recognize facial expressions and emotions. Using a mirror, children can observe their own faces as they make different expressions, enhancing self-awareness and emotional intelligence.

How It's Done:

1. **Provide a Mirror:**
   - Use a large, child-safe mirror at eye level.
   - Ensure the mirror is securely mounted or held.
2. **Explore Facial Movements:**
   - Encourage your child to make various faces:
     - Happy: Big smile.
     - Sad: Frown and downturned mouth.
     - Angry: Furrowed brow.
     - Surprised: Wide eyes and open mouth.

- Silly: Sticking out tongue, puffing cheeks.
3. **Play Copycat Games:**
    - Take turns making expressions and have the other person mimic them.
    - Use emotion cards to prompt specific expressions.
4. **Discuss Emotions:**
    - Talk about times when they have felt each emotion.
    - Ask how certain expressions make them feel inside.
5. **Extend the Activity:**
    - Sing songs or recite rhymes that involve facial movements.
    - Incorporate the mirror into dress-up play with costumes and face paint.

Benefits:

- **Emotional Awareness:** Recognizing and naming emotions.
- **Self-Expression:** Understanding how feelings are reflected in facial expressions.
- **Social Skills:** Improves empathy and the ability to read others' emotions.
- **Language Development:** Expands vocabulary related to feelings.
- **Confidence Building:** Comfort with one's own appearance and expressions.

Toys and Tools Used:

- **Mirror:** Child-safe and appropriately sized.
- **Emotion Cards (Optional):** Visual aids depicting different expressions.
- **Props (Optional):** Hats, glasses, or costumes for added fun.

Mirror play can be particularly beneficial for children who struggle with social cues. It provides a safe space to explore and understand emotions. Incorporating stories or role-playing scenarios can deepen the learning experience. Always ensure the mirror is safe and supervise the activity to guide discussions appropriately.

79. Gardening Together

Experience the joys of nature by **Gardening Together**. Planting seeds, watering plants, and watching them grow can teach children about responsibility, life cycles, and the environment while engaging their senses.

How It's Done:

1. **Choose Suitable Plants:**
   - Select easy-to-grow seeds like beans, sunflowers, or herbs.
   - Consider the available space—outdoor garden, balcony pots, or indoor planters.
2. **Prepare the Gardening Area:**
   - Gather pots, soil, trowels, and watering cans.
   - Set up a designated area for planting.
3. **Plant the Seeds:**
   - Show your child how to fill the pots with soil.
   - Plant the seeds at the appropriate depth.
   - Label the plants with their names or draw pictures.
4. **Care for the Plants:**
   - Establish a routine for watering and checking on the plants.
   - Discuss the needs of plants—sunlight, water, and nutrients.
5. **Observe Growth:**
   - Measure the plants regularly.
   - Keep a growth journal with drawings or photos.
   - Harvest and taste any edible plants, like herbs or vegetables.

Benefits:

- **Sensory Engagement:** Touching soil, smelling plants, and observing growth.
- **Responsibility:** Caring for living things fosters a sense of accountability.
- **Scientific Understanding:** Learning about plant life cycles and environmental needs.
- **Fine Motor Skills:** Planting and handling tools enhance coordination.
- **Patience and Perseverance:** Watching plants grow over time teaches delayed gratification.

Toys and Tools Used:

- **Gardening Tools:** Child-sized trowel, watering can, gloves.
- **Containers or Garden Beds:** Pots, planters, or garden plots.
- **Seeds or Seedlings:** Appropriate for the climate and season.
- **Labels and Markers:** For identifying plants.
- **Growth Journal (Optional):** Notebook for recording observations.

Gardening can be adapted to any space, even a windowsill. It's an opportunity to teach about ecology, nutrition, and where food comes from. Involving children in composting or recycling garden waste can further expand their environmental awareness. Celebrating milestones, like the first sprout or flower, can make the experience more rewarding.

80. Balloon Volleyball

Promote physical activity and coordination with a game of **Balloon Volleyball**. Using a balloon instead of a ball makes the game safer and easier for children to hit and track, providing a fun way to exercise indoors or outdoors.

How It's Done:

1. **Set Up the Playing Area:**
   - Clear a space free from obstacles.
   - Use a rope, string, or tape to mark a "net" at an appropriate height.
2. **Inflate a Balloon:**
   - Choose a brightly coloured balloon for visibility.
   - Ensure it's properly tied to prevent deflation during play.
3. **Explain the Rules:**
   - Players stand on opposite sides of the net.
   - The goal is to hit the balloon over the net without letting it touch the ground.
   - You can play cooperatively, aiming to keep the balloon in the air as long as possible, or competitively, scoring points when the other side misses.
4. **Begin the Game:**
   - Serve the balloon by tossing it into the air toward the opponent.
   - Encourage gentle hits to maintain control.
5. **Adapt as Needed:**
   - For younger children, eliminate the net and simply pass the balloon back and forth.
   - Use multiple balloons for added challenge and excitement.

Benefits:

- **Gross Motor Skills:** Enhances coordination, balance, and reflexes.

- **Hand-Eye Coordination:** Tracking and hitting the balloon improves visual-motor integration.
- **Physical Activity:** Encourages movement and exercise.
- **Social Skills:** Teaches turn-taking, cooperation, and sportsmanship.
- **Emotional Expression:** Provides an outlet for energy and can elevate mood.

Toys and Tools Used:

- **Balloon:** Latex or mylar, depending on allergies and preferences.
- **Net Substitute:** Rope, string, or tape to mark the dividing line.
- **Open Space:** Indoors with high ceilings or outdoors.
- **Optional Scoreboard:** For keeping track during competitive play.

Always supervise balloon play, especially with younger children, to prevent choking hazards if the balloon pops. You can theme the game by drawing faces or patterns on the balloon or by playing music to add energy. Balloon volleyball is easily adaptable and can be a delightful way to engage children in active play.

These activities continue to offer a range of sensory experiences, developmental benefits, and enjoyable moments for children with autism, ADHD, and Asperger's. Each one is designed to be accessible and customizable, allowing caregivers to tailor the experience to their child's unique interests and needs. Through these engaging activities, children can explore the world around them, develop important skills, and, most importantly, have fun.

81. Nature Collage Craft

Engage your child's creativity and connection with the environment by making a **Nature Collage Craft**. This activity involves collecting natural items like leaves, flowers, twigs, and pebbles to create a unique piece of art. It's an excellent way to explore textures, colours, and patterns found in nature while fostering an appreciation for the outdoors.

How It's Done:

1. **Go on a Nature Walk:**
   - Take a leisurely walk in a park, garden, or your backyard.

- Collect a variety of natural items such as leaves of different shapes and sizes, flower petals, small stones, pinecones, and twigs.
- Ensure all collected items are safe and do not harm living plants or wildlife.

2. **Prepare the Workspace:**
   - Set up a table with a large piece of paper or cardboard as the collage base.
   - Provide glue sticks, child-safe scissors, and any additional decorative materials like ribbons or stickers.

3. **Design the Collage:**
   - Encourage your child to arrange the natural items on the base without gluing them initially.
   - Discuss their placement choices and the patterns or images they want to create.

4. **Assemble the Artwork:**
   - Once satisfied with the layout, help your child glue the items onto the base.
   - They can layer materials for a 3D effect or create specific scenes like a forest, garden, or abstract designs.

5. **Add Finishing Touches:**
   - Optionally, add labels, descriptions, or drawings to complement the collage.
   - Allow the collage to dry completely before displaying it.

Benefits:

- **Sensory Exploration:** Touching and manipulating natural materials engage tactile senses.
- **Creative Expression:** Fosters imagination and artistic skills.
- **Fine Motor Skills:** Handling small items enhances dexterity and hand-eye coordination.
- **Environmental Awareness:** Encourages appreciation for nature and discussions about plants and ecosystems.
- **Language Development:** Describing materials and the creative process expands vocabulary.

Toys and Tools Used:

- **Natural Materials:** Leaves, flowers, twigs, stones, pinecones.
- **Collage Base:** Paper, cardboard, or poster board.
- **Adhesives:** Glue sticks or non-toxic liquid glue.
- **Craft Supplies (Optional):** Scissors, ribbons, stickers, markers.
- **Protective Covering:** Tablecloth or newspapers to keep the area clean.

This activity can be themed according to seasons—for example, using colourful autumn leaves or spring flowers. It also provides an opportunity to teach about respecting nature by only taking items that have fallen to the ground and ensuring no harm to the environment. Displaying the finished collage can boost your child's confidence and provide a beautiful decoration for your home.

82. Interactive Sensory Wall

Create an **Interactive Sensory Wall** in your home or classroom by mounting various sensory materials at your child's height. This tactile wall invites exploration and can be customized with different textures, colours, and interactive elements to stimulate multiple senses.

How It's Done:

1. **Select a Wall Space:**
   - Choose a safe, accessible area where you can attach materials without damaging the surface.
   - Alternatively, use a large piece of plywood or foam board that can be propped up or mounted.
2. **Gather Sensory Materials:**
   - **Textures:** Soft fabrics, sandpaper, bubble wrap, faux fur, foam shapes.
   - **Interactive Elements:** Zippers, buttons, Velcro strips, spinning wheels, light switches (non-functional).
   - **Visuals:** Mirrors, colourful patterns, LED lights.
3. **Assemble the Sensory Wall:**
   - Securely attach each item to the wall or board using strong adhesives, screws, or Velcro, ensuring there are no loose parts.
   - Arrange materials at varying heights and positions to encourage reaching and movement.
4. **Introduce the Wall to Your Child:**
   - Guide them through the different elements, demonstrating how to touch, press, or manipulate each one.
   - Encourage independent exploration while supervising for safety.
5. **Update Regularly:**
   - Swap out materials or add new elements periodically to maintain interest and address evolving sensory needs.

Benefits:

- **Sensory Stimulation:** Engages touch, sight, and sometimes sound.
- **Fine and Gross Motor Skills:** Manipulating small parts and reaching across the wall enhances coordination.
- **Exploration and Curiosity:** Promotes independent discovery and learning.
- **Emotional Regulation:** Provides a calming activity that can help manage sensory-seeking behaviors.
- **Customized Learning Tool:** Tailored to your child's specific sensory preferences and developmental goals.

Toys and Tools Used:

- **Variety of Materials:** Textures, interactive components, visual elements.
- **Mounting Supplies:** Adhesives, Velcro, screws (ensure safety).
- **Base Surface:** Wall space, plywood, or foam board.
- **Safety Features:** Rounded edges, non-toxic materials, secure attachments.

Always consider your child's safety and sensory sensitivities when selecting materials. Involve them in choosing or creating elements for the wall to increase engagement. This sensory wall can serve as a therapeutic tool, especially for children who benefit from tactile input and sensory integration activities.

---

83. Shadow Tracing Art

Combine art and science with **Shadow Tracing Art**. Using sunlight or a lamp, children can trace the shadows of objects or their own hands to create unique drawings. This activity enhances fine motor skills and teaches about light and shadows in an interactive way.

How It's Done:

1. **Set Up the Light Source:**
   - On a sunny day, position a table near a window where sunlight casts clear shadows.

- Alternatively, use a bright lamp or flashlight in a dim room to create shadows.

2. **Choose Objects for Tracing:**
   - Gather items with interesting shapes like toy animals, action figures, plants, or geometric blocks.
   - You can also use your child's hands or body parts for larger shadows.

3. **Prepare the Drawing Surface:**
   - Place a sheet of paper on the table where the shadow falls.
   - Tape the paper down to prevent it from moving.

4. **Begin Tracing:**
   - Position the object so its shadow appears on the paper.
   - Have your child trace the outline of the shadow with a pencil.
   - Encourage them to add details or colour in the shapes afterward.

5. **Experiment with Angles and Sizes:**
   - Move the light source or object to see how the shadow changes.
   - Discuss how distance and angle affect the size and shape of shadows.

Benefits:

- **Fine Motor Skills:** Tracing improves hand-eye coordination and pencil control.
- **Scientific Concepts:** Introduces principles of light, shadows, and perspective.
- **Creative Expression:** Allows for artistic embellishment of traced outlines.
- **Problem-Solving:** Experimenting with shadows fosters curiosity and critical thinking.
- **Visual Perception:** Enhances understanding of shapes and spatial relationships.

Toys and Tools Used:

- **Light Source:** Sunlight, lamp, or flashlight.
- **Objects for Tracing:** Toys, household items, hands.
- **Paper and Drawing Materials:** Pencils, markers, crayons.
- **Table and Chair:** Comfortable workspace.
- **Tape:** To secure paper.

This activity can be extended by creating a story with the traced figures or turning the shapes into imaginative creatures. It's also an opportunity to teach about the Earth's rotation and how shadows change throughout the day. Always supervise the use of lamps or flashlights to ensure safety.

84. Sensory Bottle Discovery

Craft **Sensory Bottles** filled with various materials for visual and auditory stimulation. These sealed bottles can contain glitter, beads, small toys, or liquids of different colours and viscosities, providing a calming and engaging sensory tool for children.

How It's Done:

1. **Collect Clear Bottles:**
   - Use clean, transparent plastic bottles with secure lids.
   - Bottles of different shapes and sizes add variety.
2. **Choose Fillings:**
   - **Visual Materials:** Glitter, sequins, coloured beads, water beads, small shells.
   - **Liquids:** Water with food colouring, oil, or a mix of oil and water for layering effects.
   - **Themes:** Create themed bottles like ocean (blue water, shells), space (black water, silver glitter), or rainbow (layers of coloured liquids).
3. **Assemble the Sensory Bottles:**
   - Fill the bottles with the chosen materials.
   - Leave some space at the top to allow movement.
   - Secure the lid tightly; consider gluing it shut to prevent spills.
4. **Explore Together:**
   - Shake, roll, or turn the bottles to observe the movement inside.
   - Encourage your child to describe what they see and hear.
5. **Use as Calming Tools:**
   - Sensory bottles can help soothe children when they're feeling overwhelmed.
   - They can serve as a focus object during relaxation exercises.

Benefits:

- **Visual and Auditory Stimulation:** Engages sight and sound senses.
- **Emotional Regulation:** Can have a calming effect during stress or anxiety.

- **Fine Motor Skills:** Handling the bottles improves coordination.
- **Language Development:** Describing the contents enhances vocabulary.
- **Scientific Exploration:** Observing how materials interact introduces basic physics concepts.

Toys and Tools Used:

- **Clear Plastic Bottles:** With tight-fitting lids.
- **Fillings:** Glitter, beads, small toys, coloured liquids.
- **Adhesives:** Glue or tape to seal lids securely.
- **Optional Decorations:** Stickers, labels, or ribbons.

Always supervise the creation and use of sensory bottles to ensure safety, especially with small parts. These bottles are portable and can be taken on car rides or used in various settings to provide comfort. Personalizing the bottles allows children to express their creativity and take ownership of their calming tool.

85. Paper Plate Musical Instruments

Turn simple materials into a symphony with **Paper Plate Musical Instruments**. Children can create tambourines, drums, or shakers using paper plates, beans, and craft supplies. This activity combines art, music, and fine motor skills development.

How It's Done:

1. **Gather Materials:**
   - **For Tambourines/Shakers:** Two sturdy paper plates, dried beans or rice, stapler or glue, decorations.
   - **For Drums:** One paper plate or an empty container, balloons or parchment paper, rubber bands.
2. **Assemble the Instruments:**
   - **Tambourine/Shaker:**
     - Place a handful of beans or rice between two paper plates.
     - Secure the edges with staples or strong glue, ensuring no gaps.
   - **Drum:**

- Stretch a balloon (with the end cut off) or parchment paper over the open end of a container.
- Secure it with a rubber band.

3. **Decorate:**
   o Use markers, stickers, paint, or glitter to personalize the instruments.
   o Encourage creativity with colours and designs.

4. **Make Music:**
   o Show your child how to shake the tambourine or tap the drum.
   o Experiment with different rhythms and volumes.

5. **Explore Musical Concepts:**
   o Discuss loud vs. soft sounds, fast vs. slow beats.
   o Introduce simple songs or create new ones together.

Benefits:

- **Fine Motor Skills:** Crafting the instruments enhances dexterity.
- **Auditory Stimulation:** Producing and listening to sounds engages hearing.
- **Creative Expression:** Personalizing instruments fosters artistic skills.
- **Rhythm and Timing:** Playing along with beats develops musical awareness.
- **Emotional Outlet:** Music can be a means of expressing feelings.

Toys and Tools Used:

- **Paper Plates and Containers:** As the instrument base.
- **Fillings:** Dried beans, rice, small beads.
- **Craft Supplies:** Markers, stickers, paint, glue.
- **Fasteners:** Stapler, rubber bands.
- **Optional Accessories:** Bells, ribbons.

Supervise the use of small items to prevent choking hazards. This activity can be expanded into a family band, encouraging social interaction and cooperation. Recording your musical sessions allows for playback and appreciation of your child's efforts.

86. Sensory Pathway at Home

Design an indoor **Sensory Pathway** using tape, mats, and household items to create a series of movement-based activities. This pathway encourages gross motor skills, balance, and sensory input, providing an energetic and engaging experience.

How It's Done:

1. **Plan the Pathway:**
   - Map out a safe route through a hallway or large room.
   - Include different stations with specific movements or sensory experiences.
2. **Create the Pathway Elements:**
   - **Hopscotch:** Use tape to mark squares on the floor for hopping.
   - **Balance Beam:** Place a strip of tape or a pool noodle to walk along.
   - **Jumping Pads:** Set cushions or mats for jumping between.
   - **Spin Zone:** Mark an area for spinning safely.
   - **Textured Walkway:** Lay down materials like bubble wrap, foam mats, or tactile rugs to walk over.
3. **Add Instructions:**
   - Use signs or symbols to indicate the action at each station.
   - Incorporate numbers, letters, or shapes for educational reinforcement.
4. **Guide Your Child:**
   - Walk through the pathway together initially.
   - Encourage them to follow the sequence independently.
5. **Modify Regularly:**
   - Change the order or add new elements to maintain interest.
   - Adjust the difficulty level based on your child's abilities.

Benefits:

- **Gross Motor Skills:** Enhances coordination, balance, and muscle strength.
- **Sensory Integration:** Combines movement with tactile input.
- **Cognitive Development:** Following sequences and instructions improves thinking skills.
- **Physical Activity:** Provides exercise and helps expend energy.
- **Fun and Engagement:** Makes indoor play dynamic and enjoyable.

Toys and Tools Used:

- **Tape:** For marking paths and boundaries.
- **Household Items:** Cushions, mats, bubble wrap.

- **Craft Supplies:** Signs, markers, paper for instructions.
- **Open Space:** Ensure the area is clear of obstacles.

Customize the pathway to suit your child's interests, such as a superhero training course or a journey through space. This activity can be particularly beneficial on days when outdoor play isn't possible. Always supervise to ensure safety during movement activities.

87. Visual Scavenger Hunt

Organize a **Visual Scavenger Hunt** to enhance observation skills and attention to detail. Provide a list of items or images for your child to find around the house or in the neighborhood, turning exploration into an exciting game.

How It's Done:

1. **Prepare the Scavenger Hunt List:**
   - Create a list of items to find, which can be written descriptions or pictures for non-readers.
   - Examples include "something red," "a round object," "a picture of a cat," or specific household items.
2. **Explain the Rules:**
   - Set boundaries for where the items can be found.
   - Encourage safety, reminding them not to touch fragile items without assistance.
3. **Start the Hunt:**
   - Give your child the list and a bag or basket to collect small items.
   - For larger items or things that can't be moved, they can point them out or take photos if possible.
4. **Assist as Needed:**
   - Provide hints or guidance if your child is having difficulty.
   - Celebrate each find to maintain enthusiasm.
5. **Discuss the Findings:**
   - Review the items together.
   - Ask questions about where they found them and what they observed.

Benefits:

- **Visual Perception:** Enhances the ability to notice and differentiate details.
- **Attention and Focus:** Encourages sustained concentration on a task.
- **Problem-Solving Skills:** Finding items requires thinking and strategy.
- **Language Development:** Describing items and locations expands vocabulary.
- **Confidence Building:** Successfully completing the hunt boosts self-esteem.

Toys and Tools Used:

- **Scavenger Hunt List:** Written or pictorial.
- **Bag or Basket:** For collecting items.
- **Camera (Optional):** For photographing finds.
- **Rewards (Optional):** Stickers or small prizes.

This activity can be adapted for various environments, including outdoors, during car rides, or in educational settings. You can theme the scavenger hunt around holidays, seasons, or educational topics like colours, shapes, or letters. Adjust the difficulty level to match your child's age and abilities.

88. Sensory Water Bead Play

Introduce your child to the unique texture of **Water Beads**. These small, gel-like spheres expand in water and provide a captivating sensory experience. Playing with water beads can enhance tactile exploration and fine motor skills.

How It's Done:

1. **Prepare the Water Beads:**
   - Purchase non-toxic water beads from a craft or toy store.
   - Soak them in a large bowl of water for several hours or overnight until fully expanded.
2. **Set Up the Play Area:**
   - Place the hydrated water beads in a large container or sensory bin.
   - Lay down a protective mat or towel to catch any spills.
3. **Provide Tools and Toys:**

- Include scoops, spoons, funnels, and small containers for pouring and transferring.
- Add waterproof toys like plastic animals or figurines for imaginative play.
4. **Supervise and Engage:**
   - Encourage your child to touch and manipulate the beads.
   - Discuss how they feel—slippery, squishy, smooth.
5. **Ensure Safety:**
   - Remind your child that water beads are not edible.
   - Always supervise to prevent ingestion, especially with younger children.

Benefits:

- **Tactile Sensory Input:** Engages the sense of touch with a unique texture.
- **Fine Motor Skills:** Scooping and transferring beads improve hand coordination.
- **Colour Recognition:** If using multicoloured beads, it reinforces colour identification.
- **Calming Effect:** The sensory experience can be soothing and stress-relieving.
- **Imaginative Play:** Incorporates storytelling and creative scenarios.

Toys and Tools Used:

- **Water Beads:** Non-toxic and safe for sensory play.
- **Container:** Large bin or tub.
- **Utensils:** Scoops, spoons, funnels.
- **Toys (Optional):** Waterproof figurines or objects.
- **Protective Covering:** To protect floors or tables.

Water beads can be reused if stored properly. For added educational value, you can incorporate science concepts by discussing absorption and hydration. Dispose of water beads responsibly, as they can pose environmental hazards if not handled correctly.

89. Puppet Making and Theater

Combine crafting and storytelling by **Making Puppets and Performing a Puppet Show**. Children can create their own characters and bring them to life through performance, enhancing creativity, language skills, and confidence.

How It's Done:

1. **Create Puppets:**
   - Use socks, paper bags, wooden spoons, or popsicle sticks as bases.
   - Provide craft supplies like googly eyes, yarn, felt, markers, and glue for decoration.
   - Encourage your child to design characters—people, animals, fantastical creatures.
2. **Set Up a Puppet Theater:**
   - Use a cardboard box turned on its side, a tabletop with a cloth drape, or simply perform behind a couch.
   - Decorate the theater with curtains or signs.
3. **Develop a Story:**
   - Brainstorm a storyline or adapt a favorite fairy tale.
   - Outline the sequence of events and the roles of each puppet.
4. **Rehearse and Perform:**
   - Practice the puppet movements and voices.
   - Put on the show for family members or friends.
5. **Record or Share:**
   - Film the performance to watch later.
   - Encourage applause and positive feedback to boost confidence.

Benefits:

- **Creative Expression:** Designing puppets and stories fosters imagination.
- **Language Development:** Enhances vocabulary, sentence structure, and storytelling abilities.
- **Fine Motor Skills:** Crafting and manipulating puppets improve dexterity.
- **Social Skills:** Performing builds confidence and public speaking skills.
- **Emotional Exploration:** Characters can express feelings, helping children understand emotions.

Toys and Tools Used:

- **Puppet Bases:** Socks, paper bags, wooden spoons, popsicle sticks.
- **Craft Supplies:** Glue, scissors, markers, yarn, fabric scraps.
- **Theater Setup:** Cardboard box, table, or makeshift stage.
- **Audience (Optional):** Family, friends, stuffed animals.

This activity can be tailored to individual interests, such as creating superheroes, animals, or storybook characters. It's an excellent opportunity for collaborative play if siblings or friends participate. The puppet show can become a recurring event, with new stories and characters added over time.

90. Yoga Storytime

Blend physical activity with storytelling in **Yoga Storytime**. By incorporating simple yoga poses into a narrative, children can engage their imagination while promoting flexibility, strength, and mindfulness.

How It's Done:

1. **Choose a Story or Theme:**
   - Select a favorite book, fairy tale, or create an original story.
   - Identify key elements that can be associated with yoga poses.
2. **Select Appropriate Yoga Poses:**
   - **Tree Pose:** For trees in a forest.
   - **Downward Dog:** For animals like dogs or other creatures.
   - **Cobra Pose:** For snakes or river movements.
   - **Warrior Pose:** For heroes or adventurers.
   - **Child's Pose:** For resting moments in the story.
3. **Tell the Story with Movement:**
   - Narrate the story, pausing to demonstrate and hold poses that correspond to the plot.
   - Encourage your child to mimic the poses and participate actively.
4. **Engage with Questions:**
   - Ask open-ended questions to involve your child in the storytelling.
   - "What do you think happens next?"
   - "How does our character feel now?"
5. **Conclude with Relaxation:**
   - Finish with a calming pose like savasana (lying down) and deep breathing.
   - Reflect on the story and the movements performed.

Benefits:

- **Physical Development:** Improves flexibility, balance, and muscle tone.
- **Mind-Body Connection:** Enhances awareness of bodily sensations and movements.

- **Language and Listening Skills:** Following the story and instructions boosts comprehension.
- **Imagination and Creativity:** Storytelling fosters creative thinking.
- **Emotional Regulation:** Deep breathing and movement can reduce stress and anxiety.

Toys and Tools Used:

- **Yoga Mat or Soft Surface:** For comfort and safety.
- **Book or Story Outline:** To guide the session.
- **Visual Aids (Optional):** Pictures of poses or story elements.
- **Calming Music (Optional):** To enhance the atmosphere.

Yoga storytime can be adapted to various themes like a safari adventure, space exploration, or underwater journey. This activity encourages a holistic approach to well-being, integrating physical exercise with mental and emotional development. It's suitable for individual or group settings and can become a cherished routine.

These activities aim to enrich the lives of children with autism, ADHD, and Asperger's by providing diverse sensory experiences and opportunities for growth. Each activity is thoughtfully designed to be engaging, educational, and adaptable to individual needs, fostering an environment where every child can thrive and enjoy the wonders of play and exploration.

91. Edible Sensory Play with Jelly

Dive into a squishy, wobbly world with **Edible Sensory Play using Jelly**. This activity lets children explore textures, colours, and tastes in a safe and engaging way. Using flavored gelatin, you can create a vibrant sensory bin that's perfect for little ones who love to touch and taste everything.

How It's Done:

1. **Prepare the Jelly:**
   o Choose a variety of flavored gelatin mixes in different colours.

- o Follow the package instructions to make the jelly.
- o Pour the jelly into a large, shallow container or multiple smaller containers for different colours.
- o Refrigerate until set, usually about 4 hours.

2. **Set Up the Sensory Bin:**
   - o Place the container(s) on a table or the floor with a protective mat underneath.
   - o Provide tools like spoons, spatulas, small cups, and cookie cutters.
   - o Optionally, hide edible treats like fruit pieces or gummy candies within the jelly for added surprise.

3. **Engage in Play:**
   - o Encourage your child to touch, squeeze, and scoop the jelly.
   - o They can mix colours, make shapes with cookie cutters, or simply enjoy the sensation of the jelly slipping through their fingers.
   - o Allow them to taste the jelly and discover any hidden treats.

4. **Enhance the Experience:**
   - o Discuss the different colours and flavors.
   - o Talk about the texture—ask them how it feels and what they like about it.
   - o Incorporate counting or sorting by having them separate colours or shapes.

Benefits:

- **Sensory Exploration:** Engages touch, sight, and taste.
- **Fine Motor Skills:** Manipulating tools and jelly improves hand coordination.
- **Language Development:** Encourages descriptive language and communication.
- **Cognitive Skills:** Sorting and counting enhance basic math concepts.
- **Safe and Edible:** Ideal for children who might put materials in their mouths.

Toys and Tools Used:

- **Flavored Gelatin:** Various colours and flavors.
- **Container:** Large, shallow bin or tray.
- **Utensils:** Spoons, spatulas, cups, cookie cutters.
- **Edible Add-ins:** Fruit pieces, gummy candies.

For an added educational twist, create themes like "Under the Sea" with blue jelly and fish-shaped gummies or "Dinosaur Dig" with green jelly and edible dinosaur shapes. Always supervise the activity to ensure safety and accommodate any dietary restrictions.

92. Sound and Light Show with DIY Rainsticks and Flashlights

Combine auditory and visual stimulation by creating a **Sound and Light Show** using homemade rainsticks and flashlights. This activity merges crafting with sensory play, allowing children to experience soothing sounds and engaging light patterns.

How It's Done:

1. **Create the Rainstick:**
    o Gather a cardboard tube (like a paper towel roll), aluminum foil, rice or small beads, and decorative materials.
    o Coil a long piece of aluminum foil into a spring shape and insert it into the tube.
    o Seal one end of the tube with sturdy paper or cardboard and tape.
    o Pour rice or beads into the tube.
    o Seal the other end securely.
    o Decorate the exterior with paints, stickers, or coloured tape.
2. **Prepare the Flashlights:**
    o Use small, child-friendly flashlights.
    o Optionally, attach coloured cellophane over the lens to create different light effects.
3. **Set Up the Environment:**
    o Dim the lights in the room to enhance the visibility of the flashlight beams.
    o Ensure the space is safe for movement.
4. **Engage in the Sound and Light Show:**
    o Have your child gently tilt the rainstick to hear the soothing sounds of the beads cascading inside.
    o Encourage them to move the flashlight in patterns, observing how the light interacts with surfaces.
    o Combine the two by moving the flashlight in rhythm with the rainstick sounds.
5. **Explore and Discuss:**
    o Talk about the sounds—are they like rain, a waterfall, or something else?

- Observe how the light changes when moving the flashlight closer or farther from objects.
- Experiment with shadows and reflections.

Benefits:

- **Auditory Stimulation:** The rainstick provides calming sounds.
- **Visual Engagement:** Flashlights create interesting light patterns and shadows.
- **Fine Motor Skills:** Crafting the rainstick and manipulating the flashlight enhance coordination.
- **Creative Expression:** Allows for imaginative play and storytelling.
- **Sensory Integration:** Combines multiple senses for a rich experience.

Toys and Tools Used:

- **Rainstick Materials:** Cardboard tube, aluminum foil, rice/beads, decorative items.
- **Flashlights:** Small, safe for children to handle.
- **Optional Materials:** Coloured cellophane, reflective objects.

You can expand the activity by incorporating music or creating a narrative, such as a rainforest adventure. This activity is also a great way to introduce basic science concepts about sound and light.

93. Balloon Rockets Experiment

Explore the basics of physics with a **Balloon Rockets Experiment**. This activity demonstrates principles of action and reaction in a fun, hands-on way. Children will love seeing how they can make a balloon zoom across the room using air pressure.

How It's Done:

1. **Gather Materials:**
   - Balloons (long ones work best, but round ones are fine).
   - String or fishing line.
   - Straws (plastic or paper).

- Tape.
- Two anchor points (like chairs or doorknobs).

2. **Set Up the Rocket Path:**
    - Tie one end of the string to a stationary object.
    - Thread a straw onto the string.
    - Stretch the string across the room and tie the other end to another anchor point, keeping it taut.

3. **Prepare the Balloon Rocket:**
    - Inflate a balloon but do not tie the end; hold it closed.
    - Tape the balloon to the straw on the string.
    - Position the balloon at one end of the string.

4. **Launch the Rocket:**
    - Let go of the balloon's end and watch it propel itself along the string as the air escapes.

5. **Experiment:**
    - Try different sizes and shapes of balloons.
    - Adjust the angle of the string to see how it affects speed.
    - Time the rocket's travel and record results.

Benefits:

- **Scientific Understanding:** Introduces concepts of propulsion, air pressure, and Newton's Third Law of Motion.
- **Problem-Solving Skills:** Encourages hypothesizing and experimenting with variables.
- **Fine Motor Skills:** Handling balloons and setting up the experiment improves coordination.
- **Excitement for Learning:** Engages children with a dynamic, interactive activity.

Toys and Tools Used:

- **Balloons:** Various sizes and shapes.
- **String/Fishing Line:** Long enough to span the desired distance.
- **Straws:** One per rocket setup.
- **Tape:** To attach the balloon to the straw.
- **Stopwatch (Optional):** For timing.

This activity can be turned into a friendly competition by seeing whose balloon rocket goes the fastest or the farthest. It's an excellent opportunity to introduce scientific recording methods, like charting the results of each trial.

94. Sensory Play with Shaving Cream and Sand

Combine textures for a unique tactile experience with **Shaving Cream and Sand Sensory Play**. Mixing these two materials creates a moldable, sandy foam that's fascinating to touch and manipulate. It's perfect for creative play and sensory exploration.

How It's Done:

1. **Gather Materials:**
   o Clean play sand (available at craft or hardware stores).
   o Non-menthol, unscented shaving cream.
   o Large container or sensory bin.
   o Optional: Food colouring, small toys, molds, or scoops.
2. **Prepare the Mixture:**
   o Pour sand into the container.
   o Gradually add shaving cream, mixing with hands or a spoon until it reaches a moldable consistency.
   o Adjust the amounts to achieve the desired texture—more shaving cream for fluffiness, more sand for firmness.
3. **Add Colour (Optional):**
   o Mix in a few drops of food colouring for visual appeal.
   o Knead thoroughly to distribute the colour evenly.
4. **Engage in Play:**
   o Encourage your child to squeeze, mold, and shape the sandy foam.
   o Use molds to create sandcastles or other shapes.
   o Hide small toys within the mixture for a treasure hunt.
5. **Discuss Sensations:**
   o Talk about how the mixture feels—gritty, soft, fluffy.
   o Explore how it holds shapes and compare it to regular sand or shaving cream alone.

Benefits:

- **Tactile Stimulation:** Engages the sense of touch with contrasting textures.
- **Fine Motor Development:** Manipulating the mixture enhances dexterity.
- **Creative Play:** Provides a medium for building and imaginative scenarios.
- **Language Skills:** Describing the experience expands vocabulary.

- **Sensory Integration:** Helps children process different sensory inputs simultaneously.

Toys and Tools Used:

- **Play Sand:** Clean and safe for handling.
- **Shaving Cream:** Non-toxic, unscented.
- **Container:** Large bin or tray.
- **Accessories:** Molds, scoops, small toys.
- **Protective Covering:** To make cleanup easier.

This mixture is easy to clean up—simply rinse tools and surfaces with water. Always supervise the activity to prevent ingestion and be mindful of any skin sensitivities. This sensory play can be a relaxing activity that also encourages creativity.

95. Colour Mixing with Ice Cubes

Discover the magic of colours with **Colour Mixing using Ice Cubes**. This activity allows children to explore how primary colours blend to create secondary colours while enjoying the sensory experience of melting ice.

How It's Done:

1. **Prepare Coloured Ice Cubes:**
   - Fill an ice cube tray with water.
   - Add a few drops of food colouring to each compartment—use red, blue, and yellow.
   - Freeze until solid.
2. **Set Up the Activity:**
   - Provide a large tray or shallow container.
   - Place white paper towels or a white cloth at the bottom to highlight the colours.
   - Gather the coloured ice cubes and place them in separate bowls.
3. **Begin Mixing:**
   - Let your child choose two different coloured ice cubes and place them on the tray.
   - As the ice melts, observe how the colours blend to form new hues.

o Encourage them to predict what colour will result from each combination.
4. **Experiment:**
   o Mix different combinations to see all the possible secondary colours.
   o Try adding a third colour to see how it changes the result.
   o Discuss the melting process and how temperature affects the ice.

Benefits:

- **Colour Recognition:** Teaches primary and secondary colours.
- **Scientific Concepts:** Introduces states of matter—solid ice melting into liquid water.
- **Sensory Experience:** Engages touch with the cold temperature and wet textures.
- **Critical Thinking:** Encourages making predictions and observing outcomes.
- **Fine Motor Skills:** Handling slippery ice cubes improves coordination.

Toys and Tools Used:

- **Ice Cube Tray:** For freezing coloured water.
- **Food Colouring:** Primary colours.
- **Tray or Container:** To contain the melting ice.
- **White Background:** Paper towels or cloth.
- **Bowls:** For holding ice cubes.

This activity is best done in a warm area to facilitate melting. For added fun, freeze small objects inside the ice cubes, like plastic letters or beads, to discover as the ice melts. Always supervise to manage the mess and ensure safety.

96. Bubble Painting Art

Create vibrant artwork with **Bubble Painting**, a fun activity that combines art and science. Children blow coloured bubbles onto paper, resulting in unique patterns and designs. It's an exciting way to explore colours and textures.

How It's Done:

1. **Prepare the Bubble Mixture:**
   - In small cups or bowls, mix equal parts of bubble solution (or water with dish soap) and washable liquid watercolour or food colouring.
   - Use different colours in separate containers.
   - Provide straws for blowing bubbles.
2. **Set Up the Workspace:**
   - Cover the table with a protective cloth or newspapers.
   - Use thick paper or cardstock to absorb the paint without tearing.
3. **Create Bubble Art:**
   - Have your child gently blow into the coloured bubble mixture using a straw, creating bubbles that rise above the rim of the cup.
   - Place the paper over the bubbles to capture the pattern.
   - Alternatively, blow bubbles directly onto the paper from a distance.
4. **Experiment with Techniques:**
   - Layer different colours for a multi-dimensional effect.
   - Adjust the amount of paint or soap to change bubble sizes.
   - Tilt the paper to let the colours run and blend.
5. **Safety Reminder:**
   - Instruct your child to blow out, not suck in, to avoid ingesting the mixture.
   - For younger children, consider using a bubble blower or adding a pinhole in the straw to prevent inhalation.

Benefits:

- **Artistic Expression:** Encourages creativity and exploration of colour blending.
- **Fine Motor Skills:** Blowing bubbles and handling materials enhance coordination.
- **Understanding Cause and Effect:** Observing how actions create different patterns.
- **Sensory Engagement:** Visual stimulation from colours and patterns.

Toys and Tools Used:

- **Bubble Solution:** Store-bought or homemade with dish soap and water.
- **Liquid Watercolours or Food Colouring:** To tint the bubbles.
- **Straws:** For blowing bubbles.
- **Paper:** Thick enough to handle moisture.
- **Protective Materials:** Table coverings, aprons.

Bubble painting can be themed for holidays or seasons by choosing appropriate colours. The finished artworks can be used as greeting cards, gift wrap, or decorations. Ensure that all materials are non-toxic and washable for easy cleanup.

---

97. Nature Sensory Bin

Bring the outdoors inside with a **Nature Sensory Bin**. Fill a container with natural materials like pine cones, leaves, rocks, and sticks, allowing children to explore textures, smells, and sights from nature. This activity fosters a connection with the environment and stimulates multiple senses.

How It's Done:

1. **Collect Natural Items:**
   - During a walk, gather safe, non-toxic materials such as:
     - Pine cones
     - Smooth stones
     - Leaves of various shapes and colours
     - Small sticks or twigs
     - Acorns or seed pods
   - Ensure all items are clean and free from pests.
2. **Prepare the Sensory Bin:**
   - Use a large container or tray.
   - Place all the collected items inside.
3. **Enhance the Experience:**
   - Add scoops, magnifying glasses, or tweezers for exploration.
   - Include small animal figures or insects to create imaginative play scenarios.
4. **Engage with the Materials:**
   - Encourage your child to touch and examine each item.
   - Discuss the textures—rough, smooth, prickly.
   - Talk about where each item comes from and its role in nature.
5. **Incorporate Learning:**
   - Sort the items by size, colour, or type.
   - Count the number of each kind of object.
   - Create stories or scenes using the materials.

Benefits:

- **Sensory Stimulation:** Engages touch, sight, and smell.
- **Environmental Education:** Teaches about nature and ecology.
- **Fine Motor Skills:** Handling small objects improves dexterity.
- **Cognitive Development:** Sorting and classifying enhance thinking skills.
- **Language Skills:** Discussing materials expands vocabulary.

Toys and Tools Used:

- **Natural Materials:** Collected safely from the environment.
- **Container:** Large bin or tray.
- **Exploration Tools:** Magnifying glass, scoops, tweezers.
- **Figurines (Optional):** Small animals or insects.

Always supervise to ensure that materials are handled safely and not ingested. This activity can be adapted seasonally, using different natural items available at various times of the year. It provides a tactile connection to nature, especially valuable for children who may have limited outdoor access.

98. Edible Necklaces with Cereal and Licorice

Combine crafting and snacking by making **Edible Necklaces** using cereal loops and licorice strings. This activity promotes fine motor skills as children thread cereal onto licorice, resulting in a tasty accessory they can wear and eat.

How It's Done:

1. **Gather Ingredients:**
   - Cereal loops (like Froot Loops or Cheerios).
   - Long, thin licorice strings or fruit strips.
   - Alternatively, use yarn or string if edibility is less important (ensure supervision to prevent ingestion of non-food items).
2. **Prepare for Threading:**
   - Cut licorice strings to the desired necklace length.
   - Tie a knot at one end or attach a cereal piece to prevent others from sliding off.
3. **Thread the Cereal:**
   - Show your child how to slide cereal loops onto the licorice.
   - Encourage patterns by using different colours.

- Count each piece as it's added for an educational element.

4. **Secure the Necklace:**
   - Once complete, tie the ends together to form a necklace.
   - Ensure it's loose enough to be comfortable and safe to wear.

5. **Enjoy:**
   - Let your child wear their creation.
   - They can snack on the cereal when desired.

Benefits:

- **Fine Motor Skills:** Threading enhances hand-eye coordination and pincer grasp.
- **Pattern Recognition:** Creating colour patterns promotes cognitive development.
- **Counting Skills:** Incorporates basic math through counting pieces.
- **Creative Expression:** Allows personalization and creativity.
- **Sensory Experience:** Engages taste and touch.

Toys and Tools Used:

- **Cereal Loops:** Edible and colourful.
- **Licorice Strings or Fruit Strips:** Flexible and edible threading material.
- **Alternative Threading Material:** Yarn or string (with supervision).

This activity is ideal for parties or group settings. Be mindful of any food allergies, particularly gluten or food colouring sensitivities. Always supervise young children to prevent choking hazards.

99. Light Table Exploration

Engage in a visual and tactile experience with **Light Table Exploration**. Using a light table or a DIY version, children can explore colours, shapes, and patterns with translucent materials. It's a captivating way to learn about light and colour mixing.

How It's Done:

1. **Set Up a Light Table:**

- If you don't have a light table, create one using a clear plastic storage box.
- Place battery-operated push lights or string lights inside the box.
- Cover the lights with a sheet of parchment paper or thin white cloth to diffuse the light.
- Secure the lid and flip the box over so the flat side is on top.

2. **Gather Translucent Materials:**
   - Coloured plastic shapes or tiles.
   - Transparent cups or containers.
   - Coloured cellophane or acetate sheets.
   - Clear marbles or gems.

3. **Explore and Create:**
   - Encourage your child to place materials on the lighted surface.
   - Observe how colours mix when overlapped.
   - Create patterns, pictures, or even simple math problems.

4. **Incorporate Learning Activities:**
   - Sort shapes or colours.
   - Build structures with translucent blocks.
   - Trace shapes onto paper placed over the materials.

5. **Discuss Observations:**
   - Talk about how light passes through different objects.
   - Experiment with opaque items to see the difference.

Benefits:

- **Visual Sensory Stimulation:** Enhances visual perception and interest.
- **Fine Motor Skills:** Manipulating small objects improves coordination.
- **Colour and Shape Recognition:** Reinforces basic concepts.
- **Scientific Understanding:** Introduces properties of light and transparency.
- **Creative Expression:** Encourages artistic design and experimentation.

Toys and Tools Used:

- **Light Table:** Store-bought or DIY version.
- **Translucent Materials:** Shapes, tiles, cellophane, gems.
- **Additional Items:** Paper, markers for tracing.

Ensure that the DIY light table is safe, with no overheating lights and secure closures. This activity can be adapted for different ages by adjusting the complexity of the tasks. It's an inviting way to learn and play, especially in a dimly lit room where the light effects are more pronounced.

100. Sensory Play with Oobleck

Discover the fascinating properties of non-Newtonian fluids with **Oobleck Sensory Play**. Oobleck is a simple mixture of cornstarch and water that behaves both like a solid and a liquid, offering a unique sensory experience.

How It's Done:

1. **Prepare the Oobleck:**
   - In a large bowl, mix 1.5 to 2 cups of cornstarch with 1 cup of water.
   - Adjust the consistency by adding more cornstarch or water as needed.
   - The mixture should feel solid when pressed but flow like a liquid when released.
   - Add a few drops of food colouring for visual appeal (optional).
2. **Set Up the Play Area:**
   - Pour the oobleck into a shallow container or tray.
   - Place it on a table covered with a protective cloth or do the activity outdoors.
3. **Explore the Substance:**
   - Encourage your child to squeeze, punch, and let the oobleck drip through their fingers.
   - Try rolling it into a ball (it will solidify under pressure) and then watch it melt in their hands.
4. **Experiment with Objects:**
   - Drop small toys or objects onto the surface and observe whether they sink or stay on top.
   - Use spoons or sticks to stir and poke the oobleck.
5. **Discuss the Science:**
   - Explain how oobleck behaves differently from typical liquids and solids.
   - Introduce terms like "non-Newtonian fluid" in simple language.

Benefits:

- **Sensory Exploration:** Engages touch with a unique texture.
- **Scientific Inquiry:** Encourages curiosity about physical properties.
- **Fine Motor Skills:** Manipulating the oobleck enhances hand strength.

- **Language Development:** Describing sensations and observations expands vocabulary.
- **Problem-Solving:** Experimenting with pressure and movement.

Toys and Tools Used:

- **Cornstarch and Water:** Basic ingredients.
- **Container:** Shallow tray or bin.
- **Optional Add-ins:** Food colouring, small toys.
- **Protective Covering:** To contain the mess.

Cleanup is easy with warm water, as oobleck dissolves and doesn't stain. However, avoid disposing of large amounts down the drain to prevent clogs— instead, let it dry and throw it in the trash. This activity is a classic science experiment that's both fun and educational.

---

101. Finger Knitting Craft

Introduce your child to the basics of knitting without needles through **Finger Knitting**. This activity uses just yarn and fingers to create chains that can be turned into bracelets, scarves, or decorative items. It's a soothing, repetitive motion that enhances fine motor skills.

How It's Done:

1. **Choose the Yarn:**
   - Select a thick, chunky yarn that's easy to handle.
   - Bright colours can make the activity more engaging.
2. **Learn the Technique:**
   - Start by securing the yarn end between the thumb and palm.
   - Weave the yarn over and under each finger, creating loops.
   - Repeat the weaving to have two rows of loops.
   - Lift the bottom loop over the top loop on each finger.
   - Continue weaving and lifting loops to create the knitted chain.
3. **Assist as Needed:**
   - Guide your child's fingers during the initial stages.
   - Provide verbal cues or demonstrations for each step.
4. **Finish the Piece:**

- Once the desired length is reached, bind off by lifting remaining loops over adjacent fingers until one loop remains.
- Pull the yarn through the final loop and tie a knot.

5. **Create Something Useful:**
   - Turn the knitted chain into a bracelet, headband, belt, or decoration.
   - Encourage your child to gift their creations to friends or family.

Benefits:

- **Fine Motor Skills:** Enhances dexterity and hand-eye coordination.
- **Concentration:** Requires focus and attention to detail.
- **Sense of Accomplishment:** Completing a project boosts confidence.
- **Mathematical Concepts:** Introduces patterns and sequences.
- **Calming Activity:** The repetitive motion can be soothing.

Toys and Tools Used:

- **Yarn:** Thick and easy to handle.
- **Hands:** No additional tools required.

Finger knitting is portable and can be done anywhere. It's suitable for older children who can follow sequential steps. This activity can also serve as an introduction to more complex knitting or crocheting in the future.

---

102. Sensory Path with Foot Massage Rollers

Create a relaxing and stimulating **Sensory Path using Foot Massage Rollers**. Children walk along a path made of different textured rollers or objects, providing tactile stimulation to the feet and promoting balance and coordination.

How It's Done:

1. **Gather Materials:**
   - Foot massage rollers, textured mats, bubble wrap, yoga mats, or rolled towels.
   - Any items that are safe to step on and provide varying textures.

2. **Set Up the Path:**
   - Lay out the materials in a line or pattern on the floor.
   - Ensure the path is stable and items are secure to prevent slipping.
3. **Guide the Experience:**
   - Have your child remove their shoes and socks.
   - Encourage them to walk slowly along the path, feeling the different textures under their feet.
   - They can walk forward, backward, or sideways to vary the experience.
4. **Add Elements (Optional):**
   - Incorporate balancing activities like standing on one foot.
   - Place visual markers or games along the path, such as stepping stones with numbers or letters.
5. **Discuss Sensations:**
   - Talk about how each surface feels—hard, soft, bumpy, smooth.
   - Ask which textures they prefer and why.

Benefits:

- **Tactile Sensory Input:** Stimulates nerve endings in the feet.
- **Gross Motor Skills:** Improves balance, coordination, and body awareness.
- **Calming Effect:** Foot massage can be relaxing and reduce stress.
- **Mindfulness:** Encourages focus on present sensations.
- **Physical Activity:** Promotes movement and exercise.

Toys and Tools Used:

- **Foot Massage Rollers:** Purchased or improvised.
- **Textured Materials:** Mats, bubble wrap, towels.
- **Safe Space:** Clear area to set up the path.

This activity can be adapted for different ages and abilities. For children who are sensitive to textures, start with softer materials and gradually introduce more variety. Always supervise to ensure safety, especially if balance is a challenge.

103. Sensory Play with Scented Playdough

Enhance traditional playdough fun by making **Scented Playdough**. Adding child-safe scents like vanilla, peppermint, or citrus makes the activity multi-sensory, engaging smell in addition to touch and sight.

How It's Done:

1. **Make Homemade Playdough:**
   - In a saucepan, mix 1 cup flour, 1/2 cup salt, 2 teaspoons cream of tartar.
   - Add 1 tablespoon vegetable oil, 1 cup water, and food colouring.
   - Cook over medium heat, stirring constantly until it forms a ball.
   - Remove from heat and let cool.
2. **Add Scents:**
   - Once cooled, knead in a few drops of food-grade essential oils or extracts (e.g., lemon, lavender, peppermint).
   - Adjust the amount based on the desired strength of the scent.
3. **Engage in Play:**
   - Provide tools like rolling pins, cookie cutters, or plastic knives.
   - Encourage your child to mold, shape, and create.
4. **Incorporate Learning:**
   - Use the playdough to form letters, numbers, or shapes.
   - Discuss the scents and associate them with corresponding objects (e.g., lemon scent with a yellow colour and lemon shape).
5. **Store Properly:**
   - Keep the playdough in an airtight container to maintain softness and scent.

Benefits:

- **Sensory Stimulation:** Engages touch, smell, and sight.
- **Fine Motor Skills:** Manipulating playdough improves dexterity.
- **Creative Expression:** Allows for imaginative play and creation.
- **Language Development:** Describing scents and creations expands vocabulary.
- **Calming Activity:** The act of kneading and the pleasant scents can reduce anxiety.

Toys and Tools Used:

- **Playdough Ingredients:** Flour, salt, cream of tartar, oil, water, food colouring.
- **Scents:** Food-grade essential oils or extracts.
- **Play Tools:** Rolling pins, cutters, molds.
- **Storage Containers:** Airtight jars or bags.

Ensure that the scents used are safe for children and avoid any known allergens. This activity can be themed—for example, using pumpkin spice scent in the fall or mint for the winter holidays.

104. Nature Weaving Craft

Combine art and nature with a **Nature Weaving Craft**. Using a homemade loom and collected natural materials, children can create a textured tapestry that celebrates the outdoors.

How It's Done:

1. **Create a Simple Loom:**
   - Use a sturdy cardboard rectangle or a wooden frame.
   - Cut notches along the top and bottom edges at equal intervals.
   - Stretch yarn or string between the notches to create the warp (vertical threads).
2. **Collect Weaving Materials:**
   - Gather flexible natural items like long grasses, thin twigs, flowers, leaves, and reeds.
   - Ensure materials are safe and non-toxic.
3. **Begin Weaving:**
   - Show your child how to weave the natural materials over and under the warp threads.
   - Alternate the pattern with each new piece.
4. **Add Creativity:**
   - Incorporate colourful yarn or ribbons if desired.
   - Arrange materials to create patterns or images.
5. **Finish the Weaving:**
   - Once complete, tie off the warp threads or secure them to the back of the loom.
   - Display the finished piece as wall art.

Benefits:

- **Fine Motor Skills:** Weaving enhances hand-eye coordination and dexterity.

- **Creative Expression:** Encourages artistic design and use of natural colours and textures.
- **Connection to Nature:** Promotes appreciation for the environment.
- **Concentration:** Requires focus and patience.
- **Cognitive Skills:** Understanding patterns and sequences.

Toys and Tools Used:

- **Loom Base:** Cardboard or wooden frame.
- **Warp Threads:** Yarn or string.
- **Natural Materials:** Grasses, twigs, flowers, leaves.
- **Optional Add-ins:** Coloured yarn, ribbons.

This activity is suitable for older children who can manage the weaving process. It can be a group activity, with each person contributing to a communal tapestry. Discuss the different materials used and their roles in nature.

105. DIY Sensory Matching Game

Create a **Sensory Matching Game** that challenges children to match pairs of items based on touch, sound, or smell. This game enhances sensory discrimination and memory skills.

How It's Done:

1. **Prepare the Materials:**
   o Collect small, identical containers like film canisters, plastic eggs, or opaque jars.
   o Ensure you have pairs of containers for matching.
2. **Fill the Containers:**
   o For a sound match:
     ▪ Fill pairs with different items like rice, beans, coins, or bells.
   o For a smell match:
     ▪ Place cotton balls soaked in various extracts or essential oils in each pair.
   o For a touch match:
     ▪ Fill with different textured materials like sand, beads, cotton, or buttons.

3. **Seal the Containers:**
    - o Securely close the containers to prevent peeking or spilling.
    - o Label the bottoms discreetly for answer checking.
4. **Play the Game:**
    - o Mix up the containers.
    - o Have your child shake, sniff, or feel each one to find matching pairs.
    - o Encourage them to describe what they sense.
5. **Discuss the Results:**
    - o Reveal the contents after matching.
    - o Talk about why certain items sound, smell, or feel similar or different.

Benefits:

- **Sensory Discrimination:** Enhances the ability to differentiate sensory input.
- **Memory Skills:** Strengthens recall and matching abilities.
- **Language Development:** Describing sensations expands vocabulary.
- **Critical Thinking:** Requires attention and reasoning.
- **Fun and Engagement:** Makes learning interactive and enjoyable.

Toys and Tools Used:

- **Containers:** Identical, opaque, and sealable.
- **Filling Materials:** Varied items for sound, smell, or touch.
- **Labels:** For answer keys.

This game can be adapted for different ages by adjusting the number of pairs and complexity of the sensory cues. Always ensure that materials used are safe and that containers are securely sealed to prevent access to small parts.

106. Sensory Play with Coloured Rice

Create a vibrant **Coloured Rice Sensory Bin** where children can scoop, pour, and explore. The bright colours make the activity visually stimulating, and the texture of the rice provides tactile engagement.

How It's Done:

1. **Colour the Rice:**
   - Place uncooked white rice in ziplock bags.
   - Add a few drops of food colouring and a teaspoon of vinegar or rubbing alcohol to each bag.
   - Seal and shake the bag until the rice is evenly coloured.
   - Spread the rice out on a tray to dry completely.
2. **Set Up the Sensory Bin:**
   - Pour the dried, coloured rice into a large container or bin.
   - Layer the colours for a rainbow effect or mix them together.
3. **Provide Tools and Toys:**
   - Include scoops, funnels, measuring cups, and small containers.
   - Add items like plastic letters, numbers, or small toys to find and sort.
4. **Engage in Play:**
   - Encourage your child to scoop, pour, and let the rice run through their fingers.
   - Create games like searching for hidden objects or filling containers to specific levels.
5. **Incorporate Learning:**
   - Practice counting, sorting by colour, or measuring volumes.
   - Discuss the textures and sounds the rice makes.

Benefits:

- **Tactile Sensory Input:** Engages touch with a pleasant texture.
- **Fine Motor Skills:** Scooping and pouring enhance coordination.
- **Colour Recognition:** Reinforces identification of colours.
- **Mathematical Concepts:** Introduces measuring, counting, and volume.
- **Creative Play:** Encourages imaginative scenarios.

Toys and Tools Used:

- **Uncooked Rice:** White rice for colouring.
- **Food Colouring and Vinegar/Alcohol:** For dyeing the rice.
- **Container:** Large bin or tray.
- **Utensils:** Scoops, cups, funnels.
- **Additional Items:** Small toys, letters, numbers.

Store the coloured rice in an airtight container for repeated use. Always supervise to prevent ingestion, especially with younger children. This activity can be adapted for thematic play, such as using green rice for a grass scene or blue for water.

107. Shadow Puppet Theater

Bring stories to life with a **Shadow Puppet Theater**. Using hand shadows or crafted puppets, children can create performances that stimulate imagination and storytelling skills.

How It's Done:

1. **Set Up the Theater:**
   - Hang a white sheet or large piece of paper as a screen.
   - Place a bright light source behind the screen, facing the audience area.
2. **Create Puppets:**
   - Cut out shapes of characters, animals, or objects from black cardstock or heavy paper.
   - Attach sticks or straws as handles.
3. **Learn Hand Shadows (Optional):**
   - Teach your child how to make hand shadow animals like a bird, dog, or rabbit.
4. **Develop a Story:**
   - Decide on a simple plot or adapt a familiar tale.
   - Assign characters and plan the sequence of events.
5. **Perform the Show:**
   - Move the puppets between the light source and the screen to cast shadows.
   - Use voices and sound effects to enhance the performance.

Benefits:

- **Imagination and Creativity:** Encourages inventive storytelling.
- **Fine Motor Skills:** Manipulating puppets improves dexterity.
- **Language Development:** Enhances expressive language and vocabulary.
- **Confidence Building:** Performing in front of others boosts self-esteem.
- **Understanding of Light and Shadows:** Introduces basic physics concepts.

Toys and Tools Used:

- **Screen:** White sheet or paper.
- **Light Source:** Lamp or flashlight.
- **Puppet Materials:** Black cardstock, sticks, glue.
- **Audience Space:** Seating area for viewers.

This activity can be enjoyed by the whole family. Recording the performance allows for sharing and reviewing. Discussing the shadows and how they change with distance and angle adds an educational dimension.

108. DIY Slime Making

Make your own **Slime** for a gooey, stretchy sensory experience. Slime can be customized with colours, glitter, or even scents, providing a fun and engaging activity.

How It's Done:

1. **Gather Ingredients:**
   - White school glue (non-toxic).
   - Baking soda.
   - Saline solution containing boric acid (contact lens solution).
   - Food colouring and glitter (optional).
2. **Mix the Slime:**
   - In a bowl, combine 4 ounces of glue with 1/2 cup of water.
   - Add food colouring and glitter if desired.
   - Stir in 1/2 teaspoon of baking soda.
   - Slowly add 1 tablespoon of saline solution while stirring.
   - Knead the mixture until it reaches the desired consistency.
3. **Play with the Slime:**
   - Stretch, squeeze, and mold the slime.
   - Experiment with adding small toys or objects to the slime.
4. **Store Properly:**
   - Keep the slime in an airtight container to prevent drying out.

Benefits:

- **Tactile Sensory Input:** Engages touch with a unique texture.
- **Scientific Exploration:** Understanding chemical reactions.

- **Fine Motor Skills:** Manipulating slime enhances hand strength.
- **Creative Expression:** Customizing slime allows for personalization.
- **Emotional Regulation:** The act of playing with slime can be calming.

Toys and Tools Used:

- **Slime Ingredients:** Glue, baking soda, saline solution.
- **Mixing Tools:** Bowl, spoon.
- **Add-ins:** Food colouring, glitter, small toys.
- **Storage Container:** Airtight jar or bag.

Ensure all ingredients are safe and supervise the activity to prevent ingestion. Slime can be themed for holidays or seasons, such as orange slime with black glitter for Halloween.

109. Sensory Scarf Pull Box

Create a **Scarf Pull Box** to delight infants and toddlers. Pulling colourful scarves from a container provides visual stimulation and fine motor practice.

How It's Done:

1. **Prepare the Box:**
   - Use an empty tissue box or a plastic wipes container with a slit opening.
   - Ensure there are no sharp edges.
2. **Fill with Scarves:**
   - Use lightweight, sheer scarves or fabric squares.
   - Tie the scarves together end-to-end and stuff them into the box, leaving one end poking out.
3. **Engage in Play:**
   - Encourage your child to pull the scarves out of the box.
   - They can enjoy the surprise of seeing new colours appear.
4. **Extend the Activity:**
   - Practice stuffing the scarves back in, enhancing coordination.
   - Play peek-a-boo or hide small toys among the scarves.

Benefits:

- **Fine Motor Skills:** Pulling and grasping improve dexterity.
- **Visual Stimulation:** Bright colours engage sight.
- **Cause and Effect Understanding:** Learning that actions produce results.
- **Sensory Exploration:** Textures and movement of the scarves.
- **Language Development:** Naming colours and describing actions.

Toys and Tools Used:

- **Container:** Tissue box or wipes container.
- **Scarves:** Lightweight, colourful fabrics.

Always supervise to prevent choking hazards. This activity is simple to set up and can be easily refreshed by changing the scarves or adding new elements.

110. Musical Water Glasses

Explore sounds and pitch with **Musical Water Glasses**. By filling glasses with different amounts of water, children can create a simple instrument to play tunes.

How It's Done:

1. **Set Up the Glasses:**
   - Line up several identical drinking glasses or jars.
   - Fill each with varying levels of water, creating different pitches.
2. **Add Colour (Optional):**
   - Drop different food colouring into each glass for visual appeal.
3. **Play the Glasses:**
   - Show your child how to gently tap the glasses with a spoon or mallet.
   - Experiment with different rhythms and notes.
4. **Learn Simple Songs:**
   - Arrange the glasses to play a familiar tune.
   - Mark the glasses with numbers or notes for guidance.
5. **Discuss Sound Concepts:**
   - Explain how the amount of water affects the pitch.
   - Introduce terms like "high" and "low" sounds.

Benefits:

- **Auditory Sensory Input:** Engages hearing with musical tones.
- **Scientific Understanding:** Teaches about sound waves and vibrations.
- **Fine Motor Skills:** Tapping requires control and coordination.
- **Creative Expression:** Encourages musical exploration.
- **Mathematical Concepts:** Understanding sequences and patterns.

Toys and Tools Used:

- **Glasses or Jars:** Identical for consistent sound.
- **Water:** Adjusted to different levels.
- **Utensil:** Spoon or mallet for tapping.
- **Food Colouring (Optional):** For visual enhancement.

Supervise to prevent breakage and ensure safety with glassware. This activity combines music and science, making learning enjoyable and interactive.

111. Sensory Walk on Different Textures

Create a **Sensory Walk** by arranging a series of mats or surfaces with various textures for your child to walk over barefoot. This activity stimulates the tactile sense and can help with sensory integration by exposing children to different sensations in a controlled environment.

How It's Done:

1. **Gather Materials:**
   - Collect materials with different textures such as bubble wrap, foam mats, grass mats, sandpaper, soft blankets, yoga mats, rubber bath mats, and artificial turf.
   - Ensure all materials are clean and safe for barefoot walking.
2. **Set Up the Pathway:**
   - Lay out the materials in a sequence on the floor, either indoors or outdoors.
   - Secure slippery materials with tape to prevent movement.
3. **Introduce the Walk:**
   - Encourage your child to remove their shoes and socks.

- Begin walking together over the different textures, discussing how each one feels.
4. **Incorporate Activities:**
   - Add obstacles like stepping over cushions or around cones.
   - Include visual cues like arrows or numbers to follow.
5. **Discuss Sensations:**
   - Ask your child to describe each texture: rough, smooth, squishy, prickly.
   - Encourage them to express preferences and any discomfort.

Benefits:

- **Tactile Sensory Stimulation:** Enhances touch perception and sensory processing.
- **Gross Motor Skills:** Improves balance, coordination, and spatial awareness.
- **Emotional Regulation:** Can be calming and help reduce sensory defensiveness.
- **Language Development:** Expands vocabulary through descriptive language.
- **Mindfulness:** Encourages being present and attentive to bodily sensations.

Toys and Tools Used:

- **Variety of Textured Materials:** Bubble wrap, mats, fabrics.
- **Safety Supplies:** Tape to secure materials.
- **Open Space:** An area free from hazards.

Customize the pathway to include favorite themes, like a jungle trail or a space walk. Always supervise to ensure safety, especially if your child is sensitive to certain textures. This activity can be repeated and modified to keep it engaging.

112. DIY Sensory Swing

Construct a **DIY Sensory Swing** at home to provide vestibular input that can help improve balance and coordination. Swings can be calming or alerting, making them versatile tools for sensory integration.

How It's Done:

1. **Choose a Location:**
   - Select a safe area with enough space, preferably with strong support beams.
   - Indoors, you might use a doorway with a pull-up bar or install a ceiling hook.
2. **Gather Materials:**
   - Use a sturdy fabric like a bedsheet, hammock material, or commercial-grade sensory swing fabric.
   - Obtain strong ropes, carabiners, and hardware designed to support weight.
3. **Assemble the Swing:**
   - Securely attach the fabric to the support using knots, carabiners, or hardware.
   - Ensure all attachments can bear the weight and movement of your child.
4. **Safety Check:**
   - Test the swing yourself before your child uses it.
   - Place padding or mats underneath as an extra precaution.
5. **Introduce the Swing:**
   - Explain how to use the swing safely.
   - Start with gentle movements, allowing your child to get comfortable.

Benefits:

- **Vestibular Input:** Stimulates the inner ear, aiding balance and spatial orientation.
- **Proprioceptive Feedback:** Movement and pressure help with body awareness.
- **Emotional Regulation:** Can be calming for anxiety or hyperactivity.
- **Physical Development:** Enhances core strength and coordination.

Toys and Tools Used:

- **Swing Materials:** Sturdy fabric, ropes, hardware.
- **Support Structure:** Secure beam, doorway bar, or ceiling hook.
- **Safety Padding:** Mats or cushions.

Always supervise your child during use. Swings can be tailored to different needs, such as cocoon swings for deep pressure or platform swings for standing balance activities.

---

113. Sensory Gel Bag Art

Create **Sensory Gel Bags** filled with hair gel and decorative items for squishy, mess-free tactile play. Children can manipulate the gel to move objects around, providing visual and tactile stimulation.

How It's Done:

1. **Prepare the Materials:**
   - Clear, sealable plastic bags (heavy-duty freezer bags work best).
   - Non-toxic hair gel.
   - Decorative items like sequins, glitter, beads, or small toys.
   - Duct tape for sealing edges.
2. **Assemble the Gel Bag:**
   - Fill the plastic bag with hair gel, leaving some air space.
   - Add decorative items inside the gel.
   - Seal the bag tightly, pushing out excess air.
   - Reinforce the sealed edges with duct tape to prevent leaks.
3. **Play and Explore:**
   - Lay the bag flat on a table or the floor.
   - Encourage your child to press, squeeze, and move the objects inside.
   - They can practice writing letters or numbers by pushing the gel aside.

Benefits:

- **Tactile Sensory Input:** Engages touch without the mess.
- **Fine Motor Skills:** Manipulating objects enhances hand strength.
- **Visual Tracking:** Watching items move improves visual skills.
- **Pre-Writing Skills:** Drawing shapes and letters prepares for handwriting.
- **Calming Activity:** Repetitive motions can reduce stress.

Toys and Tools Used:

- **Plastic Bags:** Heavy-duty, sealable.

- **Hair Gel:** Clear, non-toxic.
- **Decorative Items:** Sequins, beads, glitter.
- **Tape:** Duct tape for sealing.

Supervise to ensure the bag remains sealed. For added safety, you can double-bag the contents. Customize themes like ocean scenes with blue gel and fish shapes or outer space with black gel and star confetti.

114. DIY Scratch and Sniff Painting

Combine art and olfactory senses with **Scratch and Sniff Painting**. Using scented materials mixed with paint, children can create artworks that release pleasant smells when scratched.

How It's Done:

1. **Prepare the Paints:**
   - Mix unsweetened powdered drink mixes (like Kool-Aid) or spices (like cinnamon, cocoa) with small amounts of water to create scented paints.
   - Alternatively, add a few drops of food-grade essential oils to regular washable paints.
2. **Set Up the Workspace:**
   - Provide thick paper or cardstock.
   - Arrange the paints in separate containers to prevent scent mixing.
   - Offer brushes, sponges, or cotton swabs for painting.
3. **Create the Artwork:**
   - Encourage your child to paint freely, using different colours and scents.
   - Remind them to cover the paper well to embed the scents.
4. **Let It Dry:**
   - Allow the painting to dry completely.
   - Once dry, the scents will activate when the surface is gently scratched.
5. **Explore the Scents:**
   - Gently scratch the painting to release the aromas.
   - Discuss each scent and associate it with the corresponding colour or image.

Benefits:

- **Olfactory Stimulation:** Engages the sense of smell.
- **Creative Expression:** Enhances artistic skills.
- **Sensory Integration:** Combines visual, tactile, and olfactory senses.
- **Language Development:** Describing scents and artwork.
- **Fine Motor Skills:** Painting improves hand-eye coordination.

Toys and Tools Used:

- **Scented Materials:** Powdered drinks, spices, essential oils.
- **Painting Supplies:** Paper, brushes, containers.
- **Protective Covering:** Tablecloth or newspapers.

Ensure that all materials are safe and non-allergenic for your child. This activity can be themed around holidays or seasons, like using pumpkin spice for fall-themed paintings.

---

115. Sensory Balloon Pop Game

Play a thrilling **Balloon Pop Game** where children pop balloons filled with various sensory materials. This activity provides tactile and auditory stimulation and can be a fun way to reduce fear of loud noises.

How It's Done:

1. **Prepare the Balloons:**
   - Fill balloons with different materials such as rice, beans, confetti, or small toys.
   - Inflate the balloons and tie them securely.
   - Use different colours to indicate different fillings if desired.
2. **Set Up the Game:**
   - Attach the balloons to a wall, fence, or hang them from a string.
   - Ensure the area is safe and clear of sharp objects.
3. **Explain Safety Rules:**
   - Use blunt objects like pencils with erasers or plastic darts to pop balloons.
   - Supervise closely to prevent accidents.

4. **Play the Game:**
   - Let your child choose a balloon to pop.
   - After popping, explore the contents together.
   - Discuss the textures and sounds experienced.

Benefits:

- **Tactile Sensory Input:** Different fillings provide varied textures.
- **Auditory Stimulation:** The popping sound engages hearing.
- **Overcoming Fears:** Controlled exposure to loud sounds can reduce anxiety.
- **Fine Motor Skills:** Popping balloons requires hand-eye coordination.
- **Excitement and Fun:** Adds novelty to sensory exploration.

Toys and Tools Used:

- **Balloons:** Various sizes and colours.
- **Fillings:** Rice, beans, confetti, small toys.
- **Popping Tools:** Safe, blunt instruments.
- **Protective Area:** Open space or tarp to catch debris.

Consider your child's sensitivity to loud noises before choosing this activity. Always clean up thoroughly afterward to prevent choking hazards from small items.

116. Homemade Obstacle Course

Design a **Homemade Obstacle Course** using household items to promote physical activity, coordination, and problem-solving skills. Tailor the course to your child's abilities and interests.

How It's Done:

1. **Plan the Course:**
   - Identify safe areas indoors or outdoors.
   - Decide on obstacles like crawling under tables, jumping over cushions, balancing on a tape line, or tossing balls into a basket.
2. **Set Up Stations:**

- Use furniture, pillows, hula hoops, boxes, and other items.
- Create clear start and finish points.

3. **Explain the Course:**
   - Walk through each obstacle with your child.
   - Demonstrate movements if necessary.
4. **Add Challenges:**
   - Time each run to encourage improvement.
   - Incorporate tasks like carrying an object without dropping it.
5. **Modify as Needed:**
   - Adjust the difficulty based on your child's age and abilities.
   - Change the course layout to keep it engaging.

Benefits:

- **Gross Motor Skills:** Enhances strength, balance, and coordination.
- **Problem-Solving:** Navigating obstacles requires planning.
- **Physical Fitness:** Encourages active play.
- **Confidence Building:** Completing challenges boosts self-esteem.
- **Family Interaction:** Can involve siblings or parents for social skills.

Toys and Tools Used:

- **Household Items:** Furniture, cushions, boxes.
- **Play Equipment:** Hula hoops, balls, cones.
- **Safety Measures:** Clear space, supervision.

Create themes like a pirate adventure or superhero training to make it more exciting. Always ensure safety by checking for hazards and supervising closely.

117. Interactive Metronome Game

Use a metronome or metronome app to play an **Interactive Timing Game** that helps improve rhythm, timing, and attention. Children can clap, tap, or move in time with the beats.

How It's Done:

1. **Set Up the Metronome:**

- Use a physical metronome or download a metronome app.
- Choose a tempo that's appropriate for your child's age and ability.
2. **Introduce the Concept:**
   - Explain how the metronome ticks at a steady beat.
   - Demonstrate clapping or tapping along with the beats.
3. **Engage in Activities:**
   - **Clapping Game:** Clap hands together or with a partner on each beat.
   - **Movement Game:** Step, jump, or dance to the rhythm.
   - **Instrument Play:** Use drums or shakers to keep time.
4. **Adjust the Tempo:**
   - Increase or decrease the speed to challenge your child.
   - Practice starting and stopping on cue.
5. **Incorporate Songs:**
   - Sing simple songs while keeping time with the metronome.
   - Encourage creativity by making up rhythms.

Benefits:

- **Timing and Rhythm:** Improves auditory processing and coordination.
- **Attention and Focus:** Requires concentration to stay on beat.
- **Motor Skills:** Enhances fine and gross motor movements.
- **Mathematical Concepts:** Introduces counting and sequencing.
- **Enjoyment of Music:** Fosters musical interest.

Toys and Tools Used:

- **Metronome:** Physical device or app.
- **Instruments:** Drums, shakers, clappers.
- **Open Space:** Area for movement.

This activity can be adapted for group play, promoting social interaction. It's also beneficial for children who may struggle with timing and coordination.

118. DIY Kaleidoscope Craft

Build a **DIY Kaleidoscope** to explore colours and patterns. This craft combines creativity with visual sensory stimulation, allowing children to observe symmetrical designs as they turn the kaleidoscope.

How It's Done:

1. **Gather Materials:**
   - A cardboard tube (from paper towels or wrapping paper).
   - Reflective paper or thin plastic mirrors.
   - Clear plastic or translucent paper.
   - Beads, sequins, or small colourful objects.
   - Tape, scissors, and decorative materials.
2. **Assemble the Kaleidoscope:**
   - Cut reflective paper into three equal strips.
   - Tape the strips together to form a triangular prism, reflective side inward.
   - Insert the prism into the cardboard tube.
3. **Create the Viewing End:**
   - Cover one end of the tube with translucent paper or plastic, securing it with tape.
   - Poke a small hole in the center to look through.
4. **Add the Object Chamber:**
   - On the opposite end, place a clear plastic circle.
   - Add beads and sequins on top of the plastic.
   - Seal with another clear plastic circle, ensuring the items can move freely.
5. **Decorate the Exterior:**
   - Use paints, stickers, or markers to personalize the kaleidoscope.
6. **Explore Patterns:**
   - Look through the viewing hole and rotate the object chamber.
   - Observe the changing symmetrical patterns.

Benefits:

- **Visual Stimulation:** Enhances perception of colours and shapes.
- **Creative Expression:** Crafting allows for personalization.
- **Fine Motor Skills:** Cutting and assembling improve dexterity.
- **Understanding Symmetry:** Introduces basic geometric concepts.
- **Curiosity and Exploration:** Encourages observation and wonder.

Toys and Tools Used:

- **Cardboard Tube:** As the kaleidoscope body.
- **Reflective Material:** Paper or plastic mirrors.

- **Decorative Items:** Beads, sequins.
- **Craft Supplies:** Tape, scissors, markers.

Ensure safety when handling reflective materials and small objects. This activity can be a collaborative project, fostering teamwork and sharing.

---

119. Cooking Simple Recipes Together

Involve your child in **Cooking Simple Recipes** to teach life skills, math, and following instructions. Cooking engages multiple senses and can be a rewarding experience.

How It's Done:

1. **Choose an Easy Recipe:**
   - Options include making sandwiches, fruit salads, smoothies, or baking cookies.
   - Select something that matches your child's interests and abilities.
2. **Gather Ingredients and Tools:**
   - Prepare all necessary items in advance.
   - Ensure tools are safe for children (plastic knives, measuring cups).
3. **Read the Recipe Together:**
   - Go through each step, explaining any new terms.
   - Assign tasks appropriate for your child's skill level.
4. **Cook Together:**
   - Encourage participation in measuring, mixing, and assembling.
   - Discuss the sensory aspects: how ingredients look, feel, smell, and taste.
5. **Enjoy the Results:**
   - Share the finished product with family or friends.
   - Praise your child's contributions.

Benefits:

- **Life Skills:** Teaches practical cooking skills.
- **Mathematical Concepts:** Measuring introduces numbers and fractions.
- **Following Directions:** Enhances listening and comprehension.
- **Sensory Engagement:** Involves taste, smell, touch, and sight.

- **Confidence Building:** Completing a recipe fosters a sense of achievement.

Toys and Tools Used:

- **Cooking Utensils:** Child-safe tools.
- **Ingredients:** Based on the chosen recipe.
- **Apron and Clean Workspace:** For safety and hygiene.

Always supervise closely, especially when using heat or sharp objects. Cooking together can become a regular bonding activity that promotes healthy eating habits.

120. Emotional Thermometer Activity

Help your child recognize and express feelings with an **Emotional Thermometer**. This visual tool allows children to identify their emotional state and communicate it effectively.

How It's Done:

1. **Create the Thermometer:**
   - Draw a large thermometer on poster board or use a printable template.
   - Divide it into sections representing different emotions or intensity levels (e.g., calm, upset, angry).
2. **Label the Sections:**
   - Use colours or images to represent each emotion.
   - Include words or facial expressions for clarity.
3. **Introduce the Concept:**
   - Explain how emotions can change, just like the temperature.
   - Discuss what each level feels like and possible triggers.
4. **Use the Thermometer:**
   - Place it in a common area.
   - Encourage your child to indicate their current emotion by attaching a marker, clip, or Velcro arrow.
5. **Develop Coping Strategies:**

- o For higher emotion levels, discuss ways to cool down (deep breathing, quiet time).
- o Reinforce positive communication about feelings.

Benefits:

- **Emotional Awareness:** Helps identify and understand feelings.
- **Communication Skills:** Provides a way to express emotions non-verbally.
- **Self-Regulation:** Encourages strategies to manage emotions.
- **Visual Support:** Assists children who benefit from visual cues.

Toys and Tools Used:

- **Poster Board or Template:** For the thermometer.
- **Markers and Decorations:** To label and personalize.
- **Indicator:** Clip, arrow, or Velcro piece.

This tool can be used by the whole family to promote emotional intelligence. Regularly reviewing and updating the thermometer reinforces its use and effectiveness.

---

121. Sensory Pathway with Chalk

Create an outdoor **Sensory Pathway using Sidewalk Chalk**. Draw different activities on the pavement that encourage movement, balance, and coordination.

How It's Done:

1. **Design the Pathway:**
   - o Use chalk to draw shapes, lines, and instructions.
   - o Include activities like:
     - Hopscotch squares.
     - Swirl lines to follow.
     - Footprints or handprints for jumping or crawling.
     - Arrows indicating directions.
2. **Add Challenges:**
   - o Write action words like "spin," "jump," "stretch."

        o   Incorporate numbers or letters to step on in sequence.
3. **Guide Your Child:**
        o   Walk through the pathway together.
        o   Encourage following the instructions and movements.
4. **Repeat and Modify:**
        o   Change the pathway regularly to keep it engaging.
        o   Involve your child in creating new designs.

Benefits:

- **Gross Motor Skills:** Enhances physical coordination.
- **Sensory Integration:** Combines visual cues with movement.
- **Cognitive Development:** Following sequences and instructions.
- **Outdoor Activity:** Promotes exercise and fresh air.
- **Creativity:** Designing the pathway fosters artistic skills.

Toys and Tools Used:

- **Sidewalk Chalk:** Various colours.
- **Open Space:** Driveway, sidewalk, or playground.

This activity is versatile and can be adapted for different themes or educational goals. Ensure the area is safe from traffic and supervise young children.

122. Sensory Storytelling with Textured Books

Enhance reading time with **Textured Books** that include tactile elements. These books allow children to touch and feel different materials as part of the story.

How It's Done:

1. **Select Appropriate Books:**
        o   Choose books designed with textures, flaps, or interactive elements.
        o   Titles that incorporate various materials are ideal.
2. **Engage in Reading:**
        o   Read the story aloud, encouraging your child to touch the textures.
        o   Pause to discuss how each texture feels.

3. **Create Your Own Textured Book (Optional):**
    - Use a blank notebook or create pages with cardboard.
    - Attach different materials like sandpaper, cotton balls, fabric scraps.
    - Write a simple story or descriptions for each page.
4. **Interactive Storytelling:**
    - Encourage your child to predict what texture might come next.
    - Relate textures to real-life objects or experiences.

Benefits:

- **Sensory Stimulation:** Engages touch while reading.
- **Language Development:** Expands vocabulary and comprehension.
- **Fine Motor Skills:** Turning pages and touching materials.
- **Interest in Reading:** Makes books more engaging for tactile learners.

Toys and Tools Used:

- **Textured Books:** Store-bought or homemade.
- **Craft Supplies (if creating your own):** Cardboard, fabrics, glue.

This activity is suitable for children of various ages, especially those who benefit from multisensory learning. It can be a comforting bedtime routine or an educational session.

123. Bubble Wrap Stomp Painting

Combine movement and art with **Bubble Wrap Stomp Painting**. Children wear bubble wrap on their feet, dip them in paint, and stomp on paper to create unique artworks.

How It's Done:

1. **Prepare the Materials:**
    - Large sheets of paper or a roll of butcher paper.
    - Washable, non-toxic paints poured into shallow trays.
    - Bubble wrap cut into foot-sized pieces.
    - Tape to secure bubble wrap to feet.

2. **Set Up the Area:**
   - Lay the paper on the ground outdoors or in a space that can get messy.
   - Place the paint trays nearby.
3. **Get Ready:**
   - Attach bubble wrap to your child's feet using tape.
   - Ensure it's secure but comfortable.
4. **Create the Art:**
   - Have your child step into the paint, then onto the paper.
   - Encourage different movements: stomping, sliding, tiptoeing.
   - Experiment with different colours.
5. **Clean Up:**
   - Have a basin of soapy water and towels ready for washing feet.
   - Dispose of or recycle used materials appropriately.

Benefits:

- **Sensory Stimulation:** Combines tactile and auditory input from bubble wrap popping.
- **Gross Motor Skills:** Enhances coordination and balance.
- **Creative Expression:** Produces abstract art through movement.
- **Physical Activity:** Encourages energetic play.

Toys and Tools Used:

- **Bubble Wrap:** Foot-sized pieces.
- **Paint:** Washable and non-toxic.
- **Paper:** Large sheets or roll.
- **Tape:** To secure bubble wrap.

This activity is best done outdoors or in a space where mess is acceptable. Wear old clothes or protective aprons. It's a fun way to combine art and physical play.

---

124. Homemade Bird Feeder Craft

Make a **Homemade Bird Feeder** to attract wildlife and teach children about nature. This craft uses simple materials and promotes environmental awareness.

How It's Done:

1. **Gather Materials:**
   - Empty plastic bottles, milk cartons, or pine cones.
   - Birdseed mix.
   - String or twine for hanging.
   - Peanut butter (for pine cone feeders).
   - Scissors and markers for decoration.
2. **Create the Feeder:**
   - **Bottle Feeder:**
     - Cut openings on the sides for birds to access the seed.
     - Insert perches using sticks or pencils.
   - **Pine Cone Feeder:**
     - Spread peanut butter over the pine cone.
     - Roll it in birdseed until coated.
3. **Decorate (Optional):**
   - Personalize the feeder with drawings or stickers.
4. **Hang the Feeder:**
   - Choose a visible spot outside, preferably near a window.
   - Securely tie the feeder to a branch or hook.
5. **Observe the Birds:**
   - Watch for visiting birds.
   - Use a bird guide to identify different species.

Benefits:

- **Connection with Nature:** Encourages interest in wildlife.
- **Responsibility:** Caring for the feeder teaches stewardship.
- **Fine Motor Skills:** Crafting enhances dexterity.
- **Scientific Learning:** Introduces concepts of ecology and biology.
- **Patience and Observation:** Waiting for birds fosters attentiveness.

Toys and Tools Used:

- **Materials for Feeder:** Bottles, pine cones, birdseed.
- **Craft Supplies:** Markers, string, scissors.
- **Binoculars (Optional):** For bird watching.

Ensure peanut butter is safe for those without allergies. Refill the feeder as needed and clean periodically to maintain a healthy environment for birds.

125. Emotion Charades Game

Play **Emotion Charades** to help children recognize and express different feelings. Acting out emotions enhances social skills and empathy.

How It's Done:

1. **Prepare Emotion Cards:**
   - Write down various emotions on index cards (happy, sad, angry, surprised, scared, excited).
   - Include visual cues or emojis for younger children.
2. **Explain the Rules:**
   - One person picks a card and acts out the emotion without words.
   - Others guess which emotion is being displayed.
3. **Play the Game:**
   - Take turns acting and guessing.
   - Encourage expressive gestures and facial expressions.
4. **Discuss Each Emotion:**
   - After guessing, talk about situations that might cause that emotion.
   - Explore appropriate ways to respond to different feelings.

Benefits:

- **Emotional Intelligence:** Improves recognition of feelings in self and others.
- **Communication Skills:** Enhances non-verbal expression.
- **Social Interaction:** Promotes turn-taking and active participation.
- **Empathy Development:** Understanding emotions builds compassion.

Toys and Tools Used:

- **Emotion Cards:** Homemade or printed.
- **Space for Acting:** Open area to move freely.

Adjust the complexity based on age, adding more nuanced emotions for older children. This game can be a helpful tool in group settings or therapy sessions.

126. Water Balloon Target Toss

Combine aim and coordination with a **Water Balloon Target Toss**. Children throw water balloons at targets, which can be both fun and refreshing on a warm day.

How It's Done:

1. **Prepare the Balloons:**
   - Fill water balloons using a hose or faucet attachment.
   - Make a sufficient quantity for the activity.
2. **Set Up Targets:**
   - Use chalk to draw targets on a sidewalk or driveway.
   - Hang large sheets of paper with targets drawn on them.
   - Place buckets or hula hoops as ground targets.
3. **Explain the Game:**
   - Establish a throwing line to stand behind.
   - Assign points to different targets if desired.
4. **Start Tossing:**
   - Take turns throwing water balloons at the targets.
   - Encourage aiming and adjusting techniques.
5. **Safety Considerations:**
   - Ensure the area is clear of slip hazards.
   - Pick up balloon pieces afterward to prevent littering.

Benefits:

- **Gross Motor Skills:** Enhances throwing mechanics.
- **Hand-Eye Coordination:** Improves aim and spatial awareness.
- **Physical Activity:** Encourages movement and exercise.
- **Fun and Engagement:** Provides a playful way to cool off.

Toys and Tools Used:

- **Water Balloons:** Filled and tied securely.
- **Targets:** Chalk drawings, paper sheets, hoops.
- **Open Space:** Outdoor area suitable for water play.

This activity is ideal for groups and can be adapted into a friendly competition. Always supervise water play and consider environmental impact by cleaning up thoroughly.

127. Sensory Bin with Dried Pasta

Create a **Dried Pasta Sensory Bin** for tactile exploration. Using various shapes and sizes of pasta, children can scoop, sort, and play creatively.

How It's Done:

1. **Prepare the Pasta:**
   - Gather different types of dried pasta (penne, macaroni, shells, bowties).
   - Optionally, dye the pasta using food colouring and vinegar, then let it dry.
2. **Set Up the Bin:**
   - Place the pasta in a large container or sensory table.
   - Add scoops, funnels, measuring cups, and containers.
3. **Engage in Play:**
   - Encourage pouring, scooping, and filling activities.
   - Sort pasta by shape or colour.
   - Use pasta to create patterns or build structures.
4. **Incorporate Learning:**
   - Practice counting and basic math concepts.
   - Introduce vocabulary related to size, shape, and texture.

Benefits:

- **Tactile Sensory Input:** Engages touch with different textures.
- **Fine Motor Skills:** Manipulating small pieces improves dexterity.
- **Cognitive Development:** Sorting and counting enhance thinking skills.
- **Creative Play:** Encourages imagination and exploration.

Toys and Tools Used:

- **Dried Pasta:** Various shapes and colours.
- **Container:** Bin or table.
- **Utensils:** Scoops, cups, funnels.

Supervise to prevent ingestion, especially with small or dyed pasta. This activity is reusable—store pasta in a sealed container for future play.

128. Visual Tracking with Bubbles

Use **Bubbles** to enhance visual tracking skills. Watching and following bubbles as they float and move helps develop eye movement control.

How It's Done:

1. **Prepare Bubble Solution:**
   o Use store-bought bubbles or make your own with dish soap and water.
   o Provide bubble wands or blowers.
2. **Engage in Play:**
   o Blow bubbles for your child to watch.
   o Encourage them to follow bubbles with their eyes without moving their head.
3. **Interactive Activities:**
   o Have your child try to catch or pop bubbles gently.
   o Count the bubbles or describe their movement.
4. **Modify the Environment:**
   o Play indoors with fans to change bubble movement.
   o Go outside on a breezy day for varied patterns.

Benefits:

- **Visual Tracking:** Improves eye coordination and focus.
- **Hand-Eye Coordination:** Catching bubbles enhances motor skills.
- **Attention and Concentration:** Following bubbles requires sustained focus.
- **Sensory Enjoyment:** Bubbles provide visual and tactile stimulation.

Toys and Tools Used:

- **Bubble Solution:** Ready-made or homemade.
- **Bubble Wands:** Various sizes and shapes.

This simple activity is enjoyable for all ages. It's also a calming exercise that can help reduce stress.

129. Clay Impressions with Nature Items

Make **Clay Impressions** using natural items like leaves, shells, or pine cones pressed into clay to create textured art pieces.

How It's Done:

1. **Prepare the Clay:**
   - Use air-dry clay or salt dough.
   - Roll it out to a flat surface.
2. **Collect Natural Items:**
   - Gather leaves, flowers, shells, or other textured objects.
   - Ensure items are clean and dry.
3. **Create Impressions:**
   - Press the natural items firmly into the clay.
   - Carefully remove them to reveal the imprint.
4. **Finish the Pieces:**
   - Cut the clay into shapes using cookie cutters.
   - Poke a hole at the top if you want to hang them later.
   - Allow the clay to dry completely.
5. **Decorate (Optional):**
   - Paint the dried pieces.
   - Add string or ribbon to hang as ornaments.

Benefits:

- **Sensory Exploration:** Engages touch with textures.
- **Creative Expression:** Produces unique art.
- **Fine Motor Skills:** Pressing and shaping improve dexterity.
- **Connection with Nature:** Incorporates natural elements.

Toys and Tools Used:

- **Clay:** Air-dry or salt dough.
- **Natural Items:** Leaves, shells, etc.
- **Craft Supplies:** Paints, brushes, cutters.

This activity combines art and nature appreciation. It's suitable for various ages and can be adapted seasonally.

130. Listening Walk

Go on a **Listening Walk** to focus on auditory sensations. This mindful activity encourages children to pay attention to the sounds around them.

How It's Done:

1. **Plan the Walk:**
   - Choose a quiet, safe route like a park or nature trail.
2. **Set Expectations:**
   - Explain that the goal is to listen carefully to all the sounds.
   - Encourage minimal talking during the walk.
3. **During the Walk:**
   - Pause periodically to focus on different sounds.
   - Point out specific noises like birds chirping, leaves rustling, or distant traffic.
4. **After the Walk:**
   - Discuss the sounds heard.
   - Ask your child which sounds they liked or found interesting.

Benefits:

- **Auditory Awareness:** Enhances listening skills.
- **Mindfulness:** Promotes being present and attentive.
- **Language Development:** Describing sounds expands vocabulary.
- **Emotional Regulation:** Can be calming and reduce stress.

Toys and Tools Used:

- **Comfortable Footwear:** For walking.
- **Notebook (Optional):** To record sounds.

This activity can be repeated in different environments to compare sounds. It's also a great way to connect with nature and encourage observation skills.

131. Edible Finger Painting

Allow children to express their creativity with **Edible Finger Painting** using pudding or yogurt mixed with food colouring. This activity is safe for children who may explore materials with their mouths, providing a tactile and taste experience.

How It's Done:

1. **Prepare the Paint:**
   - Use plain yogurt or vanilla pudding as a base.
   - Divide it into small containers and add food colouring to create different colours.
   - Mix thoroughly to achieve vibrant hues.
2. **Set Up the Workspace:**
   - Cover the table with a plastic tablecloth or newspapers.
   - Provide thick paper or trays for painting.
3. **Engage in Painting:**
   - Encourage your child to use their fingers to paint on the paper.
   - Allow them to explore mixing colours and creating patterns.
4. **Safety Considerations:**
   - Ensure all materials are edible and safe for consumption.
   - Supervise to prevent excessive eating if necessary.

Benefits:

- **Sensory Exploration:** Engages touch, sight, and taste.
- **Creative Expression:** Fosters artistic skills.
- **Fine Motor Skills:** Improves hand coordination.
- **Safe Exploration:** Ideal for children who mouth objects.

Toys and Tools Used:

- **Edible Base:** Yogurt or pudding.
- **Food Colouring:** To create colours.
- **Paper or Trays:** For painting surfaces.
- **Protective Covering:** Tablecloth or newspapers.

This activity can be themed by using seasonal colours or creating holiday-specific artworks. Cleanup is easy with warm water and soap. Always check for food allergies before starting.

132. Sound Matching Game with Shakers

Develop auditory discrimination with a **Sound Matching Game** using homemade shakers filled with different materials. Children match pairs based on the sounds they produce when shaken.

How It's Done:

1. **Create Shakers:**
   - Use small, opaque containers like plastic eggs or film canisters.
   - Fill pairs of containers with different materials: rice, beans, beads, sand, coins.
   - Seal the containers securely with tape or glue.
2. **Set Up the Game:**
   - Mix up the shakers and lay them out on a table.
3. **Play the Game:**
   - Encourage your child to shake each container and listen to the sound.
   - Find matching pairs by identifying similar sounds.
4. **Increase Difficulty:**
   - Add more pairs or use materials with subtle sound differences.

Benefits:

- **Auditory Discrimination:** Enhances the ability to differentiate sounds.
- **Memory Skills:** Improves recall and matching.
- **Fine Motor Skills:** Handling small containers improves dexterity.
- **Language Development:** Describing sounds expands vocabulary.

Toys and Tools Used:

- **Containers:** Opaque and sealable.
- **Fillings:** Rice, beans, beads, sand, coins.
- **Sealing Materials:** Tape or glue.

This game can be adapted by using different themes or adding visual elements for additional matching. Always ensure containers are sealed to prevent spilling.

---

133. Sensory Play with Spaghetti

Engage in tactile exploration with **Cooked Spaghetti Sensory Play**. Adding colour to the noodles makes it visually stimulating and fun for children to touch and manipulate.

How It's Done:

1. **Prepare the Spaghetti:**
   - Cook spaghetti noodles according to package instructions.
   - Drain and rinse with cold water.
   - Divide into portions and add a few drops of food colouring to each, mixing well.
2. **Set Up the Sensory Bin:**
   - Place the coloured spaghetti into a large container or sensory bin.
   - Add tools like tongs, child-safe scissors (for cutting practice), or small toys.
3. **Engage in Play:**
   - Encourage your child to explore the textures.
   - Practice cutting the spaghetti with child-safe scissors.
   - Hide objects within the noodles for a treasure hunt.

Benefits:

- **Tactile Sensory Input:** Engages touch with a unique texture.
- **Fine Motor Skills:** Manipulating noodles and using tools enhance hand strength.
- **Colour Recognition:** Reinforces learning colours.
- **Creative Play:** Encourages imagination and open-ended exploration.

Toys and Tools Used:

- **Cooked Spaghetti:** Coloured with food dye.
- **Container:** Large bin or tray.
- **Utensils:** Tongs, scissors, cups.
- **Small Toys:** For added interest.

Ensure the spaghetti is cool before play begins. This activity is safe if ingested in small amounts but supervise to prevent excessive eating. Dispose of the spaghetti after use to maintain hygiene.

134. Magnetic Fishing Game

Create a **Magnetic Fishing Game** to develop hand-eye coordination and fine motor skills. Children use a homemade fishing rod to catch paper fish with paper clips attached.

How It's Done:

1. **Make the Fish:**
   - Cut out fish shapes from colourful cardstock or foam sheets.
   - Attach a paper clip to each fish's mouth area.
2. **Create the Fishing Rod:**
   - Use a stick or dowel as the rod.
   - Tie a string to one end.
   - Attach a magnet (like a small bar or disc magnet) to the end of the string.
3. **Set Up the Game:**
   - Place the fish on the floor or in a shallow container.
   - Optionally, label fish with numbers, letters, or colours for educational purposes.
4. **Play the Game:**
   - Encourage your child to "fish" by lowering the magnet to pick up the fish.
   - Practice counting, colour recognition, or spelling with the caught fish.

Benefits:

- **Fine Motor Skills:** Enhances coordination and control.
- **Hand-Eye Coordination:** Improves accuracy in movement.
- **Cognitive Development:** Reinforces educational concepts.
- **Problem-Solving:** Strategizing how to catch the fish.

Toys and Tools Used:

- **Cardstock or Foam Sheets:** For fish shapes.
- **Paper Clips:** Metal ones for magnetic attraction.
- **Stick or Dowel:** Fishing rod.
- **String and Magnet:** To catch fish.

Always supervise to ensure magnets are handled safely and not ingested. This game can be adapted for group play or competitive scoring to enhance social interaction.

135. Gardening with Succulents

Introduce responsibility and care for living things by **Planting Succulents** together. Succulents are hardy and require minimal maintenance, making them ideal for beginners.

How It's Done:

1. **Gather Materials:**
   - Small pots with drainage holes.
   - Succulent plants or cuttings.
   - Cactus or succulent potting soil.
   - Small gardening tools.
2. **Prepare the Pots:**
   - Fill pots with soil.
   - Make a small hole in the center.
3. **Plant the Succulents:**
   - Place the succulent in the hole.
   - Gently press the soil around the base.
4. **Decorate the Pots (Optional):**
   - Use paints, stickers, or markers to personalize the pots.
5. **Care Instructions:**
   - Place in a sunny spot.
   - Water sparingly when the soil is dry.

Benefits:

- **Responsibility:** Teaches care for living things.
- **Sensory Engagement:** Touching soil and plants stimulates tactile senses.

- **Fine Motor Skills:** Planting and decorating enhance dexterity.
- **Scientific Understanding:** Learning about plant growth and biology.

Toys and Tools Used:

- **Pots and Soil:** For planting.
- **Succulents:** Easy-care plants.
- **Gardening Tools:** Small shovel, gloves.
- **Decorating Supplies:** Paints, stickers.

Monitor the plants together to observe growth and discuss changes. Succulents can be a long-term project that instills pride in maintaining a living thing. This activity also fosters a connection with nature.

136. Story Stones

Boost creativity and storytelling skills with **Story Stones**. Painted stones with images or symbols can be used to inspire narratives and enhance language development.

How It's Done:

1. **Collect Stones:**
   - Find smooth, flat stones of various sizes.
   - Wash and dry them thoroughly.
2. **Paint Images:**
   - Use acrylic paints or paint markers to draw simple pictures: animals, weather, objects, emotions.
   - Let them dry completely.
3. **Seal the Stones (Optional):**
   - Apply a clear varnish to protect the artwork.
4. **Use for Storytelling:**
   - Place stones in a bag or box.
   - Draw stones randomly to create a story sequence.
   - Encourage your child to narrate a story using the images.

Benefits:

- **Creative Thinking:** Sparks imagination and original ideas.
- **Language Development:** Enhances vocabulary and narrative skills.
- **Fine Motor Skills:** Painting detailed images improves hand control.
- **Social Interaction:** Can be used in group settings for collaborative storytelling.

Toys and Tools Used:

- **Stones:** Smooth and clean.
- **Paints and Markers:** For decorating.
- **Storage Bag or Box:** To keep stones organized.

This activity can be customized to your child's interests, such as themes like space, animals, or fairy tales. Story stones are portable and can be used anywhere for impromptu storytelling, making them a versatile educational tool.

137. Alphabet Sensory Tray

Create an **Alphabet Sensory Tray** to help children learn letters through tactile exploration. Tracing letters in sensory materials reinforces letter recognition and writing skills.

How It's Done:

1. **Prepare the Tray:**
   - Use a shallow tray or baking sheet.
   - Fill with a thin layer of sensory material: sand, salt, sugar, or shaving cream.
2. **Provide Letter Cards:**
   - Use flashcards or write letters on cards.
   - Display one letter at a time as a visual reference.
3. **Engage in Tracing:**
   - Encourage your child to trace the letter in the tray using their finger or a paintbrush.
   - Practice saying the letter's name and sound.
4. **Expand the Activity:**
   - Move on to writing simple words or their name.
   - Use different materials for varied sensory input.

Benefits:

- **Letter Recognition:** Reinforces learning the alphabet in a multisensory way.
- **Pre-Writing Skills:** Develops muscle memory for writing letters.
- **Sensory Stimulation:** Engages touch and sight.
- **Fine Motor Skills:** Improves control and coordination necessary for handwriting.

Toys and Tools Used:

- **Tray and Material:** For tracing (sand, salt, etc.).
- **Letter Cards:** Visual reference for letters.
- **Tools:** Fingers, paintbrushes, or styluses.

This activity can be adapted for numbers, shapes, or even sight words. Sensory trays provide a low-pressure environment for practicing writing skills and can be particularly beneficial for tactile learners.

138. Texture Balloons

Create **Texture Balloons** by filling balloons with different materials for a tactile guessing game. Children squeeze the balloons and guess what's inside.

How It's Done:

1. **Prepare the Balloons:**
   - Use sturdy balloons.
   - Fill each balloon with a different material: flour, rice, beans, play dough, water beads.
   - Inflate slightly and tie securely.
2. **Label the Balloons (Optional):**
   - Number the balloons or use stickers to keep track.
3. **Play the Game:**
   - Have your child feel each balloon.
   - Guess what's inside based on texture and weight.
   - Reveal the contents after guessing.

Benefits:

- **Tactile Sensory Input:** Engages the sense of touch with varied textures.
- **Language Development:** Describing textures enhances vocabulary.
- **Cognitive Skills:** Hypothesizing and reasoning about what's inside.
- **Fine Motor Skills:** Squeezing and manipulating balloons strengthen hand muscles.

Toys and Tools Used:

- **Balloons:** Strong and durable.
- **Fillings:** Various textured materials (ensure they are safe and non-toxic).

Supervise to prevent balloons from popping and avoid small parts hazards, especially with younger children. This activity is both educational and entertaining, fostering curiosity and exploration.

139. DIY Rain Gauge

Combine science and nature by making a **DIY Rain Gauge**. Children learn about weather patterns and measurement by tracking rainfall.

How It's Done:

1. **Gather Materials:**
   - A clear plastic bottle (like a 2-liter soda bottle).
   - Scissors or a craft knife (adult use only).
   - Ruler.
   - Permanent marker.
   - Small stones or gravel.
2. **Assemble the Rain Gauge:**
   - Cut the top off the bottle (adult assistance required).
   - Place stones in the bottom for stability.
   - Invert the top part and place it into the bottom like a funnel.
   - Use the ruler to mark measurements on the side in centimeters or inches.
   - Draw a line at the top of the stones to indicate zero.
3. **Place Outside:**

o Find an open area away from overhangs and trees.
o Secure the gauge to prevent tipping over.
4. **Track Rainfall:**
   o After each rain, check the water level and record the amount.
   o Discuss findings and compare over time to observe weather patterns.

Benefits:

- **Scientific Learning:** Teaches about weather, measurement, and data collection.
- **Responsibility:** Caring for and regularly checking the gauge.
- **Math Skills:** Reading measurements and recording data.
- **Environmental Awareness:** Understanding natural phenomena and climate.

Toys and Tools Used:

- **Plastic Bottle:** For creating the gauge.
- **Tools:** Scissors (adult use), ruler, marker.
- **Stones:** For weight and stability.

Always supervise when using sharp tools. This project can lead to further exploration of meteorology and can be incorporated into a science journal or weather station project.

140. Parachute Play

Engage in group play with a **Parachute**. Using a large sheet or parachute, children can participate in various games that promote social skills and physical activity.

How It's Done:

1. **Obtain a Parachute:**
   o Use a commercially available play parachute or a large round sheet.

- o Ensure it's large enough for multiple participants to hold onto the edges.
2. **Gather Participants:**
   - o Ideal for small groups; at least two people can participate.
3. **Play Games:**
   - o **Mushroom:** Everyone lifts the parachute up high and then pulls it down behind them while sitting to create a mushroom shape.
   - o **Popcorn:** Place lightweight balls or soft toys on the parachute and shake to make them bounce.
   - o **Cat and Mouse:** One child (mouse) goes under the parachute, another (cat) on top tries to find them as everyone else moves the parachute.
4. **Safety Considerations:**
   - o Ensure clear communication and rules.
   - o Supervise to prevent accidents.

Benefits:

- **Gross Motor Skills:** Enhances strength, coordination, and motor planning.
- **Social Interaction:** Encourages teamwork, cooperation, and turn-taking.
- **Sensory Stimulation:** Visual and tactile engagement from the movement of the parachute.
- **Emotional Expression:** Promotes joy, laughter, and group bonding.

Toys and Tools Used:

- **Parachute or Large Sheet:** Sturdy and appropriate size.
- **Lightweight Balls or Soft Toys:** For interactive games.

Parachute play is versatile and can be adapted to various settings, including schools, therapy sessions, and family gatherings. It's excellent for building group cohesion and can be a fun way to encourage reluctant participants to join in.

141. Bubble Foam Sensory Play

Create **Bubble Foam** for a fun and messy sensory experience. This activity involves mixing water, soap, and food colouring to make fluffy, colourful foam.

How It's Done:

1. **Make the Foam:**
   - In a large bowl, mix 2 parts water with 1 part tear-free dish soap or baby shampoo.
   - Add a few drops of food colouring or liquid watercolour for colour.
   - Use an electric mixer or hand whisk to whip the mixture until it forms stiff peaks.
2. **Set Up the Play Area:**
   - Pour the foam into a sensory bin or large container.
   - Provide tools like spoons, cups, funnels, or toy cars.
3. **Engage in Play:**
   - Encourage your child to explore the foam with their hands.
   - They can make shapes, build foam towers, or pretend to wash toys.

Benefits:

- **Tactile Sensory Input:** Soft, fluffy texture stimulates touch.
- **Visual Stimulation:** Bright colours engage sight.
- **Fine Motor Skills:** Scooping, pouring, and manipulating foam.
- **Creative Play:** Open-ended exploration encourages imagination.

Toys and Tools Used:

- **Ingredients:** Water, tear-free soap, food colouring.
- **Container:** Sensory bin or large tray.
- **Utensils:** Spoons, cups, funnels.
- **Toys:** Waterproof items like plastic animals or cars.

This activity is best done outdoors or in an area that can get wet, like a bathroom or kitchen floor. Use towels or a plastic sheet to protect surfaces. Cleanup is easy with water, and the foam is safe for children who may get it on their skin.

---

142. Walking on a Balance Beam

Improve balance and coordination by **Walking on a Balance Beam**. This can be a simple line on the floor or a low, sturdy beam.

How It's Done:

1. **Create the Beam:**
   o Use a piece of tape on the floor to make a straight line for indoor play.
   o Alternatively, use a low wooden beam, a 2x4 board laid flat, or a balance beam if available.
2. **Introduce the Activity:**
   o Show your child how to walk heel-to-toe along the line or beam.
   o Encourage them to keep their arms out to the sides for balance.
3. **Add Challenges:**
   o **Backward Walk:** Try walking backward carefully.
   o **Object Balance:** Carry a small beanbag on their head or in their hands.
   o **Obstacle Course:** Place small objects to step over or around on the beam.

Benefits:

- **Gross Motor Skills:** Enhances balance, coordination, and core strength.
- **Concentration:** Requires focus and body awareness.
- **Physical Fitness:** Promotes active movement and control.

Toys and Tools Used:

- **Tape or Beam:** To create the path.
- **Space:** Clear area free from obstacles.
- **Props:** Beanbags, small objects for added challenge.

Ensure the beam is stable and the area around it is safe in case of falls. This activity can be incorporated into obstacle courses or used as part of a physical therapy program.

---

143. Cloud Dough Sensory Play

Make **Cloud Dough**, a soft and moldable substance made from flour and oil. It provides a unique texture that's both crumbly and packable, similar to wet sand.

How It's Done:

1. **Mix Ingredients:**
   - Combine 8 cups of all-purpose flour with 1 cup of vegetable oil or baby oil.
   - Mix thoroughly until the consistency resembles wet sand and holds shape when pressed.
2. **Set Up the Play Area:**
   - Place the cloud dough in a large bin or tray.
   - Provide molds, cookie cutters, cups, and utensils for shaping and building.
3. **Engage in Play:**
   - Encourage your child to squeeze, mold, and shape the dough.
   - Build sandcastles, form shapes, or simply enjoy the sensory experience.

Benefits:

- **Tactile Sensory Input:** Engages touch with a unique, soothing texture.
- **Fine Motor Skills:** Manipulating dough strengthens hand muscles.
- **Creative Play:** Open-ended exploration promotes imagination.
- **Calming Activity:** The sensory input can be relaxing and stress-reducing.

Toys and Tools Used:

- **Ingredients:** All-purpose flour, vegetable or baby oil.
- **Container:** Large bin or tray.
- **Utensils:** Molds, cutters, cups, spoons.

Cloud dough can be stored in an airtight container for future use. If using baby oil, ensure that children wash their hands after play and avoid ingestion. For an edible version, use vegetable oil and consider adding cocoa powder for colour and scent.

144. Simon Says Game

Play **Simon Says** to improve listening skills and following directions. This classic game involves performing actions only when preceded by the phrase "Simon says."

How It's Done:

1. **Explain the Rules:**
   - One person takes on the role of "Simon" and gives commands.
   - Players only perform the action if "Simon says" is stated before the command.
   - If a player performs an action without "Simon says," they receive a gentle reminder or fun consequence.
2. **Play the Game:**
   - Start with simple commands: "Simon says touch your toes," "Simon says hop on one foot."
   - Occasionally give a command without "Simon says" to test attentiveness.
3. **Rotate Roles:**
   - Allow different players to be "Simon" to keep the game engaging.

Benefits:

- **Listening Skills:** Enhances attention to detail and auditory processing.
- **Following Directions:** Improves ability to follow multi-step instructions.
- **Physical Activity:** Encourages movement and gross motor skills.
- **Social Interaction:** Promotes group participation and turn-taking.

Toys and Tools Used:

- **None Required:** Just participants and an open space.

Adapt the complexity of commands based on age and abilities. This game is versatile and can be played indoors or outdoors, making it a great option for quick, engaging activity.

145. Marble Painting Art

Engage your child's creativity and fine motor skills with **Marble Painting Art**. By rolling marbles dipped in paint across paper, children can create abstract designs while exploring colour mixing and movement.

How It's Done:

1. **Gather Materials:**
   - Shallow box or tray (a baking pan or cardboard lid works well).
   - Thick paper or cardstock that fits inside the tray.
   - Marbles or small balls.
   - Washable tempera paint in various colours.
   - Small bowls or cups for paint.
   - Spoons or tongs for handling marbles.
2. **Set Up the Workspace:**
   - Place the paper inside the tray.
   - Pour different paint colours into separate bowls.
3. **Begin Painting:**
   - Dip a marble into a paint colour using a spoon or tongs.
   - Place the marble on the paper in the tray.
   - Gently tilt and move the tray to roll the marble across the paper.
   - Repeat with different colours and marbles to create layered patterns.
4. **Explore Variations:**
   - Use different sizes of marbles or balls for varied effects.
   - Experiment with rolling multiple marbles at once.
   - Try adding glitter to the paint for extra sparkle.

Benefits:

- **Fine Motor Skills:** Tilting the tray enhances hand-eye coordination.
- **Creative Expression:** Encourages artistic experimentation and decision-making.
- **Understanding Cause and Effect:** Observing how movement affects paint patterns.
- **Sensory Engagement:** Combines visual stimulation with tactile movement.

Toys and Tools Used:

- **Marbles or Small Balls**
- **Tray or Shallow Box**
- **Thick Paper or Cardstock**
- **Washable Paint**
- **Spoons or Tongs**

Protect the work area with newspaper or a drop cloth to catch any spills. Once the artwork is dry, it can be displayed or used to create greeting cards or bookmarks. Always supervise to prevent marbles from becoming choking hazards.

146. DIY Sensory Bean Bag Toss

Create a fun and interactive game with a **DIY Sensory Bean Bag Toss**. Making and playing with bean bags can improve hand-eye coordination, motor skills, and provide tactile sensory input.

How It's Done:

1. **Make the Bean Bags:**
   - Cut fabric into squares (about 5x5 inches).
   - Place two squares together, right sides facing each other.
   - Sew around the edges, leaving a small opening.
   - Turn the fabric right side out.
   - Fill with dried beans, rice, or lentils.
   - Sew the opening closed.
2. **Set Up Targets:**
   - Use baskets, boxes, or draw targets on the ground with chalk.
   - Assign different point values to each target for a scoring game.
3. **Play the Game:**
   - Stand at a designated distance and toss the bean bags into the targets.
   - Keep score or play cooperatively to achieve a combined goal.
4. **Variations:**
   - Incorporate number or letter recognition by labeling targets.
   - Use different textures of fabric for sensory exploration.

Benefits:

- **Gross Motor Skills:** Improves throwing mechanics and coordination.
- **Hand-Eye Coordination:** Enhances aim and spatial awareness.
- **Sensory Input:** Handling bean bags provides tactile stimulation.
- **Math Skills:** Scoring can introduce counting and addition.

Toys and Tools Used:

- **Fabric Squares**
- **Filling Material:** Dried beans, rice, or lentils.
- **Sewing Supplies:** Needle and thread or sewing machine.
- **Targets:** Baskets, boxes, chalk drawings.

For a no-sew option, use socks filled with beans and tied off. Always ensure bean bags are securely closed to prevent spills. This game is adaptable for indoor or outdoor play and can be enjoyed individually or in groups.

147. Mirror Tracing Activity

Challenge perception and coordination with a **Mirror Tracing Activity**. By tracing shapes or patterns while only looking at a mirror reflection, children can develop fine motor skills and spatial awareness.

How It's Done:

1. **Set Up the Materials:**
   - Place a simple drawing or shape on a flat surface.
   - Position a mirror vertically at the edge of the paper, facing the child.
   - Provide a blank piece of paper next to the original.
2. **Explain the Task:**
   - The child must trace or copy the drawing onto the blank paper while only looking at the mirror image.
   - They should not look directly at their hand or the paper.
3. **Begin Tracing:**
   - Start with simple shapes like circles or squares.
   - Progress to more complex patterns or letters.
4. **Discuss the Experience:**
   - Talk about how it feels to rely on the mirror reflection.
   - Encourage persistence, as it may be challenging initially.

Benefits:

- **Fine Motor Skills:** Enhances precision and control.

- **Visual-Motor Integration:** Improves coordination between visual perception and motor actions.
- **Cognitive Flexibility:** Encourages adapting to new challenges.
- **Concentration:** Requires focus and attention to detail.

Toys and Tools Used:

- **Mirror:** A small tabletop mirror.
- **Paper and Pencils**
- **Simple Drawings or Patterns**

This activity can be turned into a game by timing how long it takes to complete or by comparing initial attempts to later ones to show improvement. It can also be a fun way to practice writing letters or numbers.

148. Emotion Bingo Game

Play **Emotion Bingo** to help children recognize and understand different facial expressions and feelings. This game promotes emotional intelligence and social skills in an interactive format.

How It's Done:

1. **Create Bingo Cards:**
   - Design bingo cards with various facial expressions representing different emotions (happy, sad, angry, surprised, etc.).
   - Ensure each card has a different arrangement of emotions.
2. **Prepare Emotion Cards:**
   - Make a set of cards or use a spinner with the same emotions depicted.
3. **Play the Game:**
   - Draw an emotion card or spin the spinner.
   - Players identify and mark the corresponding emotion on their bingo card.
   - The first to complete a row, column, or full card shouts "Bingo!"
4. **Discuss Emotions:**
   - After each round, talk about situations that might cause each emotion.

o Encourage sharing personal experiences.

Benefits:

- **Emotional Awareness:** Enhances recognition and understanding of emotions.
- **Social Skills:** Promotes interaction and communication.
- **Language Development:** Expands vocabulary related to feelings.
- **Cognitive Skills:** Improves memory and matching abilities.

Toys and Tools Used:

- **Bingo Cards:** Customized with emotion faces.
- **Markers:** Chips, tokens, or crayons to mark cards.
- **Emotion Cards or Spinner**

This game can be adapted for various ages by adjusting the complexity of the emotions depicted. It's a valuable tool for group settings, such as classrooms or therapy sessions, to facilitate discussions about feelings.

149. Musical Chairs with a Twist

Enjoy a non-competitive version of **Musical Chairs** that focuses on cooperation and fun rather than competition. This activity promotes movement, listening skills, and social interaction.

How It's Done:

1. **Set Up Chairs:**
   o Arrange chairs in a circle, one for each participant.
   o Alternatively, use cushions or mats.
2. **Play Music:**
   o Use lively, upbeat songs that children enjoy.
3. **Introduce the Twist:**
   o Instead of removing chairs, have players perform a different action when the music stops (e.g., freeze in place, make a funny face, or switch seats).
4. **Begin the Game:**

- o Start the music and have children walk or dance around the chairs.
- o When the music stops, they perform the designated action.

5. **Variations:**
   - o Assign different actions for each round.
   - o Incorporate themes, such as animal movements or dance styles.

Benefits:

- **Gross Motor Skills:** Encourages movement and coordination.
- **Listening Skills:** Requires attention to music cues.
- **Social Interaction:** Promotes inclusion and cooperation.
- **Emotional Regulation:** Helps manage excitement and impulsivity.

Toys and Tools Used:

- **Chairs or Mats:** One per participant.
- **Music Player:** Device to play and pause songs.

By removing the competitive element, this version reduces anxiety and allows all children to participate fully. It's adaptable for various group sizes and can be a fun activity for parties or gatherings.

150. Planting Seeds and Watching Them Grow

Experience the wonder of nature by **Planting Seeds** and observing their growth over time. This activity teaches patience, responsibility, and basic biological concepts.

How It's Done:

1. **Choose Seeds:**
   - o Select fast-growing plants like beans, peas, or sunflowers.
2. **Prepare the Planting Area:**
   - o Use small pots, egg cartons, or a garden bed.
   - o Fill with potting soil.
3. **Plant the Seeds:**
   - o Follow the instructions on the seed packet for depth and spacing.
   - o Water gently.

4. **Care for the Plants:**
   - Place in a sunny location.
   - Establish a routine for watering and monitoring growth.
5. **Observe and Document:**
   - Measure the plants regularly.
   - Keep a growth journal with drawings or photos.

Benefits:

- **Responsibility:** Caring for plants fosters accountability.
- **Scientific Understanding:** Introduces plant life cycles and ecology.
- **Patience and Perseverance:** Observing gradual growth teaches delayed gratification.
- **Sensory Engagement:** Involves touch, sight, and sometimes smell.

Toys and Tools Used:

- **Seeds and Soil**
- **Containers:** Pots, egg cartons, or garden space.
- **Watering Can or Spray Bottle**
- **Notebook (Optional):** For recording observations.

This activity can be extended by transplanting seedlings into a garden or larger pots. It's an opportunity to discuss topics like photosynthesis, nutrition, and environmental care. Ensure all materials are safe and appropriate for the child's age.

151. Puzzle and Problem-Solving Games

Engage your child's critical thinking with **Puzzles and Problem-Solving Games**. Activities like jigsaw puzzles, maze books, or logic games enhance cognitive development and concentration.

How It's Done:

1. **Select Appropriate Puzzles:**
   - Choose puzzles suited to your child's age and skill level.

       o Options include jigsaw puzzles, Sudoku, crosswords, or Rubik's Cubes.

2. **Create a Comfortable Workspace:**
   - o Provide a quiet area with good lighting.
   - o Use a table or flat surface for assembling puzzles.
3. **Encourage Strategies:**
   - o Show how to sort pieces by colour or edge.
   - o Discuss different approaches to solving problems.
4. **Work Together:**
   - o Collaborate on challenging puzzles.
   - o Celebrate successes to build confidence.

Benefits:

- **Cognitive Development:** Enhances problem-solving and reasoning skills.
- **Fine Motor Skills:** Manipulating pieces improves dexterity.
- **Patience and Persistence:** Teaches perseverance through challenges.
- **Visual-Spatial Skills:** Develops understanding of how pieces fit together.

Toys and Tools Used:

- **Puzzles:** Jigsaws, logic games, maze books.
- **Workspace:** Table or flat surface.
- **Organizers (Optional):** Trays or containers for sorting pieces.

Puzzles can be a solo activity or a collaborative effort. They offer a screen-free option for entertainment and learning. Start with simpler puzzles and gradually increase complexity as skills improve.

152. Building with Blocks and Legos

Stimulate creativity and engineering skills by **Building with Blocks and Legos**. Constructing structures encourages imaginative play and spatial reasoning.

How It's Done:

1. **Provide Building Materials:**

- Use wooden blocks, Lego sets, magnetic tiles, or other construction toys.

2. **Set a Theme (Optional):**
   - Challenge your child to build a specific structure like a bridge, house, or vehicle.
   - Alternatively, allow free-building to encourage creativity.

3. **Engage in Building:**
   - Join in to model building techniques or collaborate on a project.
   - Encourage storytelling around the creations.

4. **Introduce Challenges:**
   - Set time limits.
   - Use only certain colours or shapes.

Benefits:

- **Fine Motor Skills:** Enhances hand-eye coordination and precision.
- **Spatial Awareness:** Develops understanding of shapes, sizes, and balance.
- **Problem-Solving:** Encourages planning and adjusting designs.
- **Creative Expression:** Fosters imagination and innovation.

Toys and Tools Used:

- **Building Blocks:** Legos, wooden blocks, magnetic tiles.
- **Space:** Flat surface for construction.
- **Additional Materials (Optional):** Figures, vehicles for extended play.

Building activities can be adapted for individual or group play. They support STEM learning by introducing basic engineering concepts. Displaying completed projects can boost pride and encourage further exploration.

153. Colour Sorting and Matching Games

Enhance cognitive skills with **Colour Sorting and Matching Games**. Sorting objects by colour helps with classification skills and colour recognition.

How It's Done:

1. **Gather Coloured Items:**
   - Use toys, blocks, buttons, or paper cutouts in various colours.
2. **Set Up Sorting Containers:**
   - Provide bowls, trays, or sections labeled with different colours.
3. **Explain the Activity:**
   - Demonstrate how to sort items into the matching colour containers.
4. **Engage in Sorting:**
   - Encourage your child to sort all the items.
   - Discuss each colour and associated objects.
5. **Introduce Variations:**
   - Time the activity to add a challenge.
   - Sort by shades or patterns.

Benefits:

- **Colour Recognition:** Reinforces understanding of colours.
- **Cognitive Development:** Enhances categorization and organizational skills.
- **Fine Motor Skills:** Picking up and placing items improves dexterity.
- **Language Skills:** Expands vocabulary related to colours and objects.

Toys and Tools Used:

- **Coloured Objects:** Blocks, buttons, paper pieces.
- **Sorting Containers:** Bowls, trays, labeled sections.
- **Labels (Optional):** Colour names or swatches.

This activity can be adapted for shapes, sizes, or other attributes. It's suitable for younger children and can be a foundational exercise for more complex classification tasks.

154. Making a Time Capsule

Create a **Time Capsule** to preserve memories and practice planning. This project involves collecting items to be sealed away and opened at a future date.

How It's Done:

1. **Select a Container:**
   - Use a sturdy box, metal tin, or plastic container.
2. **Gather Items:**
   - Include drawings, letters to future selves, photographs, small toys, or newspaper clippings.
3. **Document the Present:**
   - Write about current favorite things, events, or personal thoughts.
4. **Seal the Capsule:**
   - Place all items in the container.
   - Seal it securely and label with the date it should be opened.
5. **Store Safely:**
   - Keep the time capsule in a safe place where it won't be disturbed.

Benefits:

- **Self-Reflection:** Encourages thinking about personal growth.
- **Planning Skills:** Involves setting future goals and anticipation.
- **Creative Expression:** Personalizes the project with meaningful items.
- **Family Engagement:** Can involve multiple family members.

Toys and Tools Used:

- **Container:** Box, tin, or jar.
- **Personal Items:** Letters, drawings, photos.
- **Writing Supplies**

Decide on an appropriate time frame for reopening the capsule (e.g., one year, five years). This activity can become a cherished tradition and provides a tangible link to the past when opened.

155. Storytelling with Puppets

Enhance language and social skills through **Storytelling with Puppets**. Creating and performing puppet shows encourages imagination and expressive communication.

How It's Done:

1. **Create Puppets:**
   - Use socks, paper bags, felt, or craft sticks.
   - Decorate with markers, yarn, buttons, and fabric scraps.
2. **Set Up a Stage:**
   - Use a tabletop, couch back, or make a simple puppet theater with a cardboard box.
3. **Develop a Story:**
   - Brainstorm a plot or adapt a favorite tale.
   - Assign characters to each puppet.
4. **Perform the Show:**
   - Encourage expressive voices and movements.
   - Invite family members to watch or participate.

Benefits:

- **Language Development:** Enhances storytelling and vocabulary.
- **Social Skills:** Promotes interaction and cooperation.
- **Creative Expression:** Fosters imagination and role-playing.
- **Confidence Building:** Performing boosts self-esteem.

Toys and Tools Used:

- **Puppet Materials:** Socks, bags, craft supplies.
- **Stage Area:** Simple setup for performances.
- **Props (Optional):** Small accessories to enhance the story.

Puppet shows can be recorded for later viewing or sharing with others. This activity is flexible and can be tailored to different themes or educational topics.

156. DIY Wind Chimes

Combine crafting and music by making **DIY Wind Chimes**. This project allows children to explore sounds and create decorative art.

How It's Done:

1. **Gather Materials:**

- Items that make pleasant sounds when struck, such as metal washers, keys, shells, small bells, or bamboo pieces.
- A sturdy stick or embroidery hoop for the base.
- String or fishing line.
- Decorative materials like beads or ribbons.

2. **Assemble the Wind Chime:**
   - Tie strings of varying lengths to the base.
   - Attach sound-making items to the ends of the strings.
   - Decorate the base and strings as desired.

3. **Hang the Wind Chime:**
   - Find a spot where the wind can catch it, like a porch or near a window.

4. **Explore the Sounds:**
   - Listen to the different tones produced.
   - Discuss how materials and lengths affect the sound.

Benefits:

- **Fine Motor Skills:** Tying knots and threading improves dexterity.
- **Creative Expression:** Designing and decorating fosters artistic skills.
- **Scientific Exploration:** Introduces concepts of sound and vibration.
- **Sensory Stimulation:** Provides auditory input from the chimes.

Toys and Tools Used:

- **Sound-Making Items:** Metal pieces, shells, bells.
- **Base:** Stick or hoop.
- **String or Fishing Line**
- **Decorations:** Beads, ribbons.

Ensure all materials are weather-resistant if placed outdoors. This activity can be connected to lessons about music, weather, or environmental sounds.

---

157. Making Homemade Instruments

Encourage musical exploration by **Making Homemade Instruments**. Crafting instruments like drums, shakers, or guitars promotes creativity and auditory skills.

How It's Done:

1. **Choose an Instrument to Make:**
   - **Drum:** Use empty cans or containers with balloons stretched over the top.
   - **Shaker:** Fill plastic bottles with rice or beans.
   - **Guitar:** Stretch rubber bands around a box or container.
2. **Decorate the Instruments:**
   - Use paint, stickers, or markers to personalize.
3. **Create Music:**
   - Experiment with different sounds.
   - Form a family band and play together.

Benefits:

- **Fine Motor Skills:** Crafting enhances hand coordination.
- **Auditory Development:** Explores different sounds and rhythms.
- **Creative Expression:** Combines art and music.
- **Social Interaction:** Encourages group participation.

Toys and Tools Used:

- **Recyclable Materials:** Cans, bottles, boxes.
- **Fillings:** Rice, beans, rubber bands.
- **Craft Supplies:** Decorations.

This activity promotes environmental awareness by reusing materials. It's adaptable to various ages and can be extended by learning simple songs or rhythms.

158. Water Play with Boats

Enjoy **Water Play with Boats** by making simple boats and floating them in a tub or pool. This activity combines crafting with sensory play and scientific exploration.

How It's Done:

1. **Create Boats:**
   - Use materials like corks, sponges, plastic bottles, or folded paper.
   - Attach sails made from toothpicks and paper.
2. **Set Up Water Area:**
   - Fill a large container, bathtub, or kiddie pool with water.
3. **Test the Boats:**
   - Place boats in the water and observe how they float.
   - Experiment with adding weight or changing designs.
4. **Add Challenges:**
   - Blow on the sails to move the boats.
   - Create currents with hands or fans.

Benefits:

- **Scientific Understanding:** Introduces concepts of buoyancy and propulsion.
- **Fine Motor Skills:** Building boats enhances dexterity.
- **Sensory Play:** Water provides tactile stimulation.
- **Problem-Solving:** Adjusting designs to improve performance.

Toys and Tools Used:

- **Boat Materials:** Corks, sponges, bottles, paper.
- **Water Container**
- **Craft Supplies:** Toothpicks, paper, glue.

Always supervise water play to ensure safety. This activity can be expanded into lessons about sea travel, weather effects on boats, or historical explorations.

159. Treasure Hunt with Clues

Organize a **Treasure Hunt** with clues leading to a hidden prize. This game promotes problem-solving, reading comprehension, and physical activity.

How It's Done:

1. **Plan the Hunt:**
   - Decide on a series of locations for clues.

- Write clues that lead from one spot to the next.
2. **Set Up Clues:**
    - Place each clue in its designated spot.
    - Use riddles, simple directions, or pictures.
3. **Hide the Treasure:**
    - Choose a final prize, like a small toy or treat.
    - Hide it at the last location.
4. **Conduct the Hunt:**
    - Provide the first clue to your child.
    - Assist as needed, encouraging independent problem-solving.

Benefits:

- **Cognitive Development:** Enhances logical thinking and comprehension.
- **Reading Skills:** Practices reading and interpreting clues.
- **Physical Activity:** Encourages movement between locations.
- **Excitement and Motivation:** Builds anticipation and engagement.

Toys and Tools Used:

- **Clue Cards:** Written or drawn.
- **Treasure:** Small prize or treat.
- **Props (Optional):** Maps, compass.

The treasure hunt can be themed (pirates, detectives) to increase interest. Adjust the complexity based on the child's age and abilities. It's a versatile activity suitable for indoors or outdoors.

160. Picture Collage Craft

Create a **Picture Collage** using cut-out images from magazines, photos, or drawings. This artistic activity encourages self-expression and fine motor skills.

How It's Done:

1. **Gather Materials:**
    - Magazines, newspapers, old photographs.
    - Scissors, glue, and a large piece of paper or poster board.

2. **Choose a Theme (Optional):**
   - Topics like "My Favorite Things," "Nature," or "Family."
3. **Cut Out Images:**
   - Select pictures that fit the theme or interest your child.
   - Practice safe scissor use.
4. **Assemble the Collage:**
   - Arrange the images on the paper.
   - Glue them in place, overlapping or spaced as desired.
5. **Add Decorations:**
   - Use markers, stickers, or glitter to enhance the collage.

Benefits:

- **Creative Expression:** Allows personal artistic choices.
- **Fine Motor Skills:** Cutting and gluing improve dexterity.
- **Visual Planning:** Arranging images develops spatial awareness.
- **Emotional Expression:** Can represent feelings or interests.

Toys and Tools Used:

- **Magazines and Photos**
- **Scissors and Glue**
- **Paper or Poster Board**
- **Decorative Supplies**

Discuss the collage afterward to encourage communication about the chosen images. This activity can be a way to explore themes or topics your child is curious about.

---

161. Dress-Up and Role Play

Encourage imagination and social skills with **Dress-Up and Role Play**. Using costumes and props, children can act out various scenarios, fostering creativity and empathy.

How It's Done:

1. **Provide Costumes and Props:**

o   Use old clothes, hats, scarves, costume jewelry.
o   Include props like toy tools, kitchen utensils, or stuffed animals.
2. **Create a Dress-Up Area:**
   o   Set up a space with a mirror and storage for costumes.
3. **Role Play Scenarios:**
   o   Suggest themes like "Superhero Adventure," "Cooking Show," or "Animal Safari."
   o   Allow your child to lead and create their own stories.
4. **Join In:**
   o   Participate as a character or audience.
   o   Encourage dialogue and interaction.

Benefits:

- **Social Skills:** Enhances communication and understanding of roles.
- **Emotional Development:** Allows expression of feelings and perspectives.
- **Language Skills:** Expands vocabulary and storytelling abilities.
- **Creative Thinking:** Fosters imagination and problem-solving.

Toys and Tools Used:

- **Costumes:** Clothes, accessories.
- **Props:** Themed items for scenarios.
- **Mirror (Optional):** For visual feedback.

Role play can be tailored to explore real-life situations, helping children process experiences like doctor visits or starting school. It's an enjoyable way to build confidence and empathy.

162. Dance Party with Freeze

Have fun and burn energy with a **Dance Party with Freeze**. Children dance to music and must freeze in place when the music stops, improving self-control and listening skills.

How It's Done:

1. **Choose Music:**
   - Select upbeat songs your child enjoys.
2. **Explain the Game:**
   - Dance while the music plays.
   - When the music stops, everyone must freeze in their current pose.
3. **Play the Game:**
   - Start and stop the music at random intervals.
   - Encourage expressive dancing and creative freeze poses.
4. **Add Challenges:**
   - Assign specific dance styles or themes.
   - Use props like scarves or ribbons.

Benefits:

- **Gross Motor Skills:** Enhances coordination and movement.
- **Listening Skills:** Requires attention to auditory cues.
- **Self-Regulation:** Practices impulse control during "freeze" moments.
- **Emotional Expression:** Allows for joyful expression through dance.

Toys and Tools Used:

- **Music Player**
- **Props (Optional):** Scarves, ribbons.

This activity is adaptable for different ages and can be played indoors or outdoors. It's a lively way to engage in physical activity and can be incorporated into parties or group settings.

163. Finger Puppet Craft and Play

Combine crafting and storytelling with **Finger Puppets**. Creating and using finger puppets promotes fine motor skills and imaginative play.

How It's Done:

1. **Make Finger Puppets:**
   - Use felt, paper, or fabric to create small puppets that fit on fingers.
   - Decorate with markers, googly eyes, and yarn.

2. **Design Characters:**
   - o Create animals, people, or fantastical creatures.
   - o Give each puppet a name and personality.
3. **Perform Puppet Shows:**
   - o Develop short stories or skits.
   - o Use a small stage or perform over a table edge.
4. **Encourage Creativity:**
   - o Allow your child to invent scenarios and dialogues.
   - o Join in to model expressive storytelling.

Benefits:

- **Fine Motor Skills:** Crafting and manipulating puppets enhance dexterity.
- **Language Development:** Expands vocabulary and narrative skills.
- **Creative Expression:** Fosters imagination and role-play.
- **Social Skills:** Encourages interaction and sharing.

Toys and Tools Used:

- **Craft Materials:** Felt, paper, fabric, decorations.
- **Glue and Scissors**
- **Performance Space**

Finger puppets are portable and can be used in various settings, such as during travel or waiting times. This activity is suitable for individual play or group interactions.

---

164. Sensory Bottle with Glitter and Oil

Create a mesmerizing **Sensory Bottle** filled with glitter, water, and oil. Shaking the bottle produces swirling patterns that can be calming and visually stimulating.

How It's Done:

1. **Prepare the Bottle:**
   - o Use a clear plastic bottle with a tight-fitting lid.
2. **Fill the Bottle:**

- Fill halfway with water.
- Add glitter, sequins, or small beads.
- Fill the remaining space with clear oil (like baby oil).

3. **Seal the Bottle:**
   - Secure the lid tightly.
   - Consider gluing the lid closed for safety.

4. **Explore the Bottle:**
   - Shake or turn the bottle to watch the contents swirl and settle.
   - Use it as a calming tool during quiet time.

Benefits:

- **Visual Sensory Input:** Provides soothing visual stimulation.
- **Emotional Regulation:** Can help calm anxiety or agitation.
- **Fine Motor Skills:** Handling the bottle improves coordination.
- **Scientific Exploration:** Observing how oil and water interact.

Toys and Tools Used:

- **Clear Plastic Bottle**
- **Water and Oil**
- **Glitter and Decorative Items**
- **Adhesive (Optional):** To seal the lid.

Customize the sensory bottle with different colours or themes. It's a simple yet effective tool for self-soothing and can be used in various environments, such as at home or in the classroom.

These activities continue to offer diverse experiences designed to support the development and enjoyment of children with autism, ADHD, and Asperger's. Each activity is thoughtfully crafted to be engaging, educational, and adaptable to individual needs, ensuring that every child can find joy and growth through these explorations.

165. Nature Scavenger Hunt

Organize a **Nature Scavenger Hunt** to encourage exploration and observation of the natural environment. This activity promotes physical activity, curiosity, and environmental awareness.

How It's Done:

1. **Prepare a List:**
   - Create a list of natural items to find, such as a smooth rock, a yellow leaf, a feather, or a pine cone.
   - Include pictures or drawings for younger children.
2. **Set Boundaries:**
   - Define the safe area for the hunt, whether it's a backyard, park, or trail.
3. **Equip Participants:**
   - Provide a small bag or basket for collecting items.
   - Offer magnifying glasses or binoculars for observation.
4. **Begin the Hunt:**
   - Give the list to your child and explore together.
   - Encourage taking time to observe and appreciate each item.
5. **Discuss Findings:**
   - After the hunt, talk about each item collected.
   - Discuss textures, colours, and the role of each item in nature.

Benefits:

- **Environmental Awareness:** Teaches about nature and ecosystems.
- **Physical Activity:** Encourages walking and exploring outdoors.
- **Observation Skills:** Enhances attention to detail.
- **Language Development:** Expands vocabulary related to nature.

Toys and Tools Used:

- **List of Items:** With words and/or pictures.
- **Collection Bag or Basket**
- **Exploration Tools:** Magnifying glass, binoculars.

Always supervise children during outdoor activities to ensure safety. This activity can be adapted for different environments and seasons. Encourage respect for nature by only collecting items that have fallen to the ground and avoiding disturbing wildlife.

166. Baking Soda and Vinegar Volcano

Create a classic **Baking Soda and Vinegar Volcano** to introduce basic chemistry concepts. This exciting experiment demonstrates chemical reactions in a visual and engaging way.

How It's Done:

1. **Build the Volcano:**
   - Use clay, playdough, or a mound of sand to form a volcano shape around a plastic bottle or cup.
   - Ensure the opening at the top is clear.
2. **Prepare the Eruption:**
   - Place the volcano on a tray or outdoor area to contain the mess.
   - Add a few tablespoons of baking soda inside the bottle.
   - Optional: Add a few drops of dish soap and red food colouring for effect.
3. **Initiate the Reaction:**
   - Pour vinegar into the bottle and step back.
   - Watch as the mixture fizzes and flows out like lava.
4. **Experiment Further:**
   - Try different amounts of baking soda and vinegar.
   - Discuss why the reaction occurs.

Benefits:

- **Scientific Learning:** Introduces chemical reactions and gases.
- **Visual Stimulation:** Engaging and memorable demonstration.
- **Fine Motor Skills:** Measuring and pouring ingredients.
- **Critical Thinking:** Encourages questioning and hypothesis testing.

Toys and Tools Used:

- **Materials for Volcano Structure:** Clay, playdough, sand.
- **Plastic Bottle or Cup**
- **Baking Soda and Vinegar**
- **Dish Soap and Food Colouring (Optional)**
- **Tray or Protective Surface**

Always supervise during the experiment to ensure safety. This activity can be a starting point for discussions about geology, volcanoes, and earth science. Cleanup is simple with water.

167. Leaf Rubbings Art

Create beautiful **Leaf Rubbings** to capture the intricate patterns of leaves. This art activity connects children with nature and enhances fine motor skills.

How It's Done:

1. **Collect Leaves:**
   - Gather leaves of various shapes and sizes.
   - Choose leaves with prominent veins for better results.
2. **Prepare Materials:**
   - Use thin paper like newsprint or regular printer paper.
   - Provide crayons with the paper wrapping removed.
3. **Create Rubbings:**
   - Place a leaf underside up on a flat surface.
   - Lay the paper over the leaf.
   - Gently rub the side of a crayon over the paper, revealing the leaf's texture.
4. **Experiment with Colours:**
   - Use different colours for layering effects.
   - Try rubbing multiple leaves on the same page for a collage.

Benefits:

- **Artistic Expression:** Encourages creativity and appreciation of natural patterns.
- **Fine Motor Skills:** Rubbing requires controlled movements.
- **Sensory Exploration:** Engages touch and sight.
- **Environmental Awareness:** Connects art with nature.

Toys and Tools Used:

- **Leaves:** Various shapes and textures.
- **Paper:** Thin and flexible.
- **Crayons:** Wrappers removed for side rubbing.

This activity can be extended by identifying the types of leaves and learning about different trees. It's suitable for all ages and can be adapted for classroom settings.

168. Balloon Tennis

Play **Balloon Tennis** to promote physical activity and coordination. Using balloons and homemade paddles, children can enjoy indoor or outdoor play.

How It's Done:

1. **Make the Paddles:**
   - Attach paper plates to sticks or wooden paint stirrers using tape or glue.
   - Decorate the plates if desired.
2. **Prepare the Balloons:**
   - Inflate balloons to a manageable size.
3. **Set Up the Game:**
   - Establish a playing area free of obstacles.
   - Use a piece of string or tape on the floor to create a "net" if desired.
4. **Play Tennis:**
   - Hit the balloon back and forth using the paddles.
   - Keep the balloon from touching the ground.

Benefits:

- **Gross Motor Skills:** Enhances movement and coordination.
- **Hand-Eye Coordination:** Improves tracking and timing.
- **Physical Fitness:** Encourages active play.
- **Social Interaction:** Promotes cooperation and turn-taking.

Toys and Tools Used:

- **Balloons**
- **Paper Plates and Sticks:** For paddles.
- **Tape or Glue**
- **Open Space**

This game can be adapted for solo play by counting how many times the balloon can be hit without touching the ground. Always supervise balloon play to prevent choking hazards with popped balloons.

169. Sensory Path with Chalk Obstacles

Design a **Chalk Obstacle Course** on pavement to combine creativity and physical activity. This activity encourages gross motor skills and imaginative play.

How It's Done:

1. **Create the Path:**
   - Use sidewalk chalk to draw different obstacles like hopscotch grids, balance lines, zigzags, and circles.
2. **Add Instructions:**
   - Write actions next to each section, such as "Jump three times," "Spin," or "Walk on tiptoes."
3. **Navigate the Course:**
   - Guide your child through the path, following the instructions.
   - Encourage them to create their own obstacles.

Benefits:

- **Physical Activity:** Promotes movement and coordination.
- **Creative Expression:** Designing the course fosters imagination.
- **Following Directions:** Enhances listening and comprehension.
- **Outdoor Engagement:** Encourages time spent outside.

Toys and Tools Used:

- **Sidewalk Chalk**
- **Pavement Area:** Driveway, sidewalk, playground.

This activity can be refreshed by changing the obstacles regularly. It can also be adapted for group play, promoting social interaction and teamwork.

170. Rock Painting and Kindness Rocks

Engage in **Rock Painting** to create decorative pieces or **Kindness Rocks** with positive messages. This craft encourages artistic skills and spreading positivity.

How It's Done:

1. **Collect Rocks:**
   - Find smooth, flat rocks suitable for painting.
   - Wash and dry them thoroughly.
2. **Paint Designs:**
   - Use acrylic paints or paint pens to decorate the rocks.
   - Create images, patterns, or write uplifting messages.
3. **Seal the Artwork:**
   - Apply a clear sealant to protect the paint if the rocks will be placed outside.
4. **Distribute Kindness Rocks (Optional):**
   - Place the rocks in public spaces for others to find.
   - Encourage discussions about kindness and community.

Benefits:

- **Artistic Expression:** Enhances creativity and fine motor skills.
- **Emotional Development:** Promotes empathy and positive thinking.
- **Community Engagement:** Connects with others through shared messages.
- **Sensory Experience:** Handling natural materials engages touch.

Toys and Tools Used:

- **Rocks:** Smooth and clean.
- **Paints and Brushes**
- **Sealant (Optional)**
- **Markers or Paint Pens**

Always seek permission if placing rocks in public areas, following local guidelines. This activity can be part of a larger community project or simply enjoyed at home.

171. Paper Airplane Competition

Host a **Paper Airplane Competition** to explore aerodynamics and encourage friendly competition. Children can design, build, and test their own paper airplanes.

How It's Done:

1. **Provide Materials:**
   o Use different types of paper: printer paper, cardstock, or recycled materials.
   o Offer stickers or markers for decoration.
2. **Design and Fold:**
   o Teach basic paper airplane folds or encourage original designs.
   o Experiment with different shapes and weights.
3. **Set Up the Competition:**
   o Mark a starting line and measure distances.
   o Categorize flights by distance, airtime, or accuracy to a target.
4. **Test and Record:**
   o Fly the airplanes and record results.
   o Discuss why some designs perform better.

Benefits:

- **Scientific Exploration:** Introduces principles of flight and physics.
- **Fine Motor Skills:** Folding and adjusting planes improves dexterity.
- **Problem-Solving:** Encourages experimentation and iteration.
- **Social Interaction:** Promotes teamwork and sportsmanship.

Toys and Tools Used:

- **Paper:** Various types.
- **Decorations:** Stickers, markers.
- **Measuring Tools:** Tape measure, stopwatch.

This activity can be expanded by researching real aircraft designs or incorporating lessons on gravity and air resistance. It's suitable for indoor or outdoor play.

172. Scarf Dancing

Combine movement and music with **Scarf Dancing**. Using lightweight scarves, children can express themselves through dance while enhancing coordination.

How It's Done:

1. **Provide Scarves:**
   - Use silk scarves, ribbon wands, or lightweight fabric strips.
2. **Select Music:**
   - Choose songs with varying tempos and styles.
3. **Dance Freely:**
   - Encourage your child to move the scarves to the rhythm.
   - Explore different movements like waving, tossing, and swirling.
4. **Introduce Themes:**
   - Suggest mimicking elements like water, wind, or animals.

Benefits:

- **Gross Motor Skills:** Enhances coordination and spatial awareness.
- **Creative Expression:** Encourages imagination and emotional expression.
- **Sensory Stimulation:** Movement with scarves provides tactile feedback.
- **Rhythm and Timing:** Develops musicality and listening skills.

Toys and Tools Used:

- **Scarves or Fabric Strips**
- **Music Player**

Scarf dancing is adaptable for all abilities and can be calming or energizing. It can also be incorporated into storytelling or educational themes.

173. Edible Playdough Making

Make **Edible Playdough** for safe, sensory play. This activity combines cooking and crafting, allowing children to create and taste their creations.

How It's Done:

1. **Prepare Ingredients:**
   o Mix 1 cup of creamy peanut butter (or sunflower seed butter for allergies), 2 cups of powdered sugar, and 1/2 cup of honey.
2. **Mix the Dough:**
   o Combine all ingredients in a bowl.
   o Knead until it reaches a playdough consistency.
3. **Engage in Play:**
   o Use cookie cutters, molds, or hands to shape the dough.
   o Decorate with edible items like chocolate chips or sprinkles.
4. **Enjoy Eating:**
   o Allow your child to taste their creations.

Benefits:

- **Sensory Exploration:** Engages touch, taste, and smell.
- **Fine Motor Skills:** Manipulating dough enhances dexterity.
- **Creative Expression:** Encourages imaginative play.
- **Safe Exploration:** Suitable for children who may put materials in their mouths.

Toys and Tools Used:

- **Ingredients:** Peanut butter (or alternative), powdered sugar, honey.
- **Utensils:** Mixing bowl, spoon.
- **Play Tools:** Cookie cutters, molds.

Always check for food allergies before choosing ingredients. Store any leftover dough in the refrigerator. This activity combines fun with a delicious treat.

174. Indoor Camping Adventure

Create an **Indoor Camping Adventure** to spark imagination and provide a change of scenery. This activity involves setting up a makeshift campsite inside your home.

How It's Done:

1. **Set Up a Tent:**
   - Use a real tent or create one with sheets and furniture.
   - Include sleeping bags or blankets inside.
2. **Create a Campfire:**
   - Make a pretend campfire using coloured paper, tissue paper, and logs.
   - Use flashlights or battery-operated candles for effect.
3. **Plan Activities:**
   - Tell stories or read books by flashlight.
   - Sing campfire songs.
   - Have a picnic with snacks.
4. **Add Camping Elements:**
   - Use binoculars to "observe" indoor wildlife.
   - Play nature sounds in the background.

Benefits:

- **Imaginative Play:** Encourages creativity and role-playing.
- **Family Bonding:** Offers quality time together.
- **Emotional Comfort:** Creates a cozy and safe environment.
- **Problem-Solving:** Involves planning and setting up the campsite.

Toys and Tools Used:

- **Tent or Sheets and Furniture**
- **Blankets and Pillows**
- **Flashlights or Battery Candles**
- **Props:** Binoculars, books, snacks.

This activity can be a special event for evenings or weekends. It provides an opportunity to disconnect from screens and engage in interactive play.

---

175. Making Salt Dough Ornaments

Craft **Salt Dough Ornaments** to create lasting keepsakes. This activity combines art and sensory play, resulting in personalized decorations.

How It's Done:

1. **Prepare the Dough:**
   - Mix 1 cup of flour, 1/2 cup of salt, and 1/2 cup of water.
   - Knead until smooth.
2. **Create Shapes:**
   - Roll out the dough on a floured surface.
   - Use cookie cutters to make shapes.
   - Poke a hole at the top if you plan to hang them.
3. **Bake the Ornaments:**
   - Place on a baking sheet and bake at 200°F (93°C) for 2-3 hours until hard.
4. **Decorate:**
   - Once cooled, paint with acrylic paints.
   - Add glitter, stickers, or other embellishments.
   - Seal with a clear varnish if desired.

Benefits:

- **Artistic Expression:** Encourages creativity and design.
- **Fine Motor Skills:** Rolling and cutting dough enhances coordination.
- **Sensory Play:** Engages touch through dough manipulation.
- **Pride in Creation:** Produces tangible items to display or gift.

Toys and Tools Used:

- **Ingredients:** Flour, salt, water.
- **Baking Supplies:** Bowl, spoon, baking sheet.
- **Cookie Cutters**
- **Decorations:** Paints, glitter.

These ornaments make great gifts and can become a yearly tradition. Always supervise baking and handle hot items with care.

176. Yoga for Kids

Introduce **Yoga for Kids** to promote physical well-being and mindfulness. Simple poses can enhance flexibility, balance, and focus.

How It's Done:

1. **Create a Calm Space:**
   - Use yoga mats or soft flooring.
   - Play gentle music if desired.
2. **Select Simple Poses:**
   - Tree Pose, Downward Dog, Cobra, Child's Pose.
   - Use visual aids or demonstration.
3. **Guide Through Poses:**
   - Explain each pose and its benefits.
   - Encourage deep breathing and concentration.
4. **Incorporate Stories:**
   - Use imaginative narratives to make poses engaging.
   - For example, "Let's be a tall tree swaying in the wind."

Benefits:

- **Physical Health:** Improves strength, flexibility, and coordination.
- **Emotional Regulation:** Teaches relaxation and stress reduction.
- **Mindfulness:** Encourages focus on the present moment.
- **Body Awareness:** Enhances understanding of body movements.

Toys and Tools Used:

- **Yoga Mats or Soft Surface**
- **Visual Aids (Optional):** Pose cards or posters.
- **Music (Optional):** Calm, soothing tunes.

Yoga sessions can be brief and adapted to the child's interest level. Consistent practice can lead to long-term benefits in physical and emotional health.

177. Magnetic Art with Metal Objects

Create **Magnetic Art** using magnets and metal objects. This activity combines science and creativity, allowing children to explore magnetism while designing patterns.

How It's Done:

1. **Gather Materials:**
   o Use a magnetic board or a cookie sheet.
   o Provide magnets, metal lids, washers, paper clips.
2. **Explore Magnetism:**
   o Demonstrate how magnets attract metal objects.
   o Allow your child to experiment freely.
3. **Create Designs:**
   o Arrange metal pieces into shapes or pictures.
   o Use magnets to hold them in place.
4. **Incorporate Challenges:**
   o Build the tallest structure possible.
   o Create specific images like faces or letters.

Benefits:

- **Scientific Understanding:** Introduces basic concepts of magnetism.
- **Fine Motor Skills:** Manipulating small objects enhances dexterity.
- **Creative Expression:** Encourages artistic design.
- **Problem-Solving:** Involves planning and adjusting designs.

Toys and Tools Used:

- **Magnetic Surface:** Board or cookie sheet.
- **Magnets and Metal Objects**
- **Safety Note:** Avoid small magnets with young children due to ingestion risk.

Always supervise the use of small magnets. This activity can lead to discussions about how magnets work and their uses in everyday life.

178. Building a Fort

Construct a **Fort** using household items. Building and playing in forts stimulates imagination and provides a cozy space for play.

How It's Done:

1. **Collect Materials:**
   o Use blankets, sheets, pillows, and furniture like chairs and tables.
2. **Design the Fort:**
   o Drape sheets over furniture to create walls and a roof.
   o Use clothespins or clips to secure fabric.
3. **Furnish the Interior:**
   o Add pillows, stuffed animals, and lighting like flashlights or fairy lights.
4. **Enjoy the Space:**
   o Use the fort for reading, playing games, or quiet time.
   o Encourage your child to personalize it.

Benefits:

- **Creative Thinking:** Planning and building enhances problem-solving.
- **Physical Activity:** Involves movement and coordination.
- **Emotional Comfort:** Provides a safe, private space.
- **Imaginative Play:** Fosters storytelling and role-playing.

Toys and Tools Used:

- **Fabric:** Blankets, sheets.
- **Furniture:** Chairs, tables.
- **Clips or Clothespins**
- **Decorations:** Pillows, lights.

Building a fort can be a collaborative family activity. It offers a change of environment without leaving home and can be a recurring activity with new designs each time.

179. Paper Plate Animals Craft

Create **Paper Plate Animals** using simple craft materials. This activity encourages creativity and fine motor skills.

How It's Done:

1. **Choose an Animal:**
   - Decide on an animal to create, such as a lion, fish, or bird.
2. **Prepare Materials:**
   - Use paper plates as the base.
   - Provide paints, markers, construction paper, googly eyes, glue, and scissors.
3. **Assemble the Animal:**
   - Paint or colour the plate to match the animal.
   - Add features like ears, fins, or wings with cut-out paper.
   - Attach eyes and other details.
4. **Display or Play:**
   - Hang the creations on the wall.
   - Use them as props for storytelling or imaginative play.

Benefits:

- **Artistic Expression:** Enhances creativity and design skills.
- **Fine Motor Skills:** Cutting and gluing improve dexterity.
- **Knowledge Building:** Learn about different animals.
- **Confidence Boosting:** Completing a craft fosters a sense of accomplishment.

Toys and Tools Used:

- **Paper Plates**
- **Craft Supplies:** Paints, markers, paper, glue, scissors.
- **Decorations:** Googly eyes, glitter.

This activity can be adapted for various themes or educational topics, such as sea creatures or jungle animals. It's suitable for individual or group settings.

180. Memory Matching Game

Play a **Memory Matching Game** to enhance cognitive skills. This classic game involves matching pairs of cards based on memory.

How It's Done:

1. **Prepare the Cards:**
   - Use a set of matching picture cards.
   - Alternatively, create your own using index cards with drawings or stickers.
2. **Set Up the Game:**
   - Shuffle the cards and lay them face down in a grid.
3. **Explain the Rules:**
   - Players take turns flipping over two cards.
   - If the cards match, the player keeps them and takes another turn.
   - If they don't match, flip them back over and the next player goes.
4. **Play the Game:**
   - Continue until all matches are found.
   - The player with the most matches wins.

Benefits:

- **Memory Skills:** Enhances short-term recall.
- **Attention to Detail:** Requires careful observation.
- **Turn-Taking:** Promotes social skills.
- **Language Development:** Discussing the images expands vocabulary.

Toys and Tools Used:

- **Matching Cards:** Store-bought or homemade.
- **Flat Surface:** Table or floor space.

Adjust the number of card pairs based on age and ability. Themes can be tailored to interests, such as animals, shapes, or letters.

181. Watercolour Resist Art

Create **Watercolour Resist Art** using crayons and watercolours. This technique reveals hidden designs when painted over, delighting children with the surprise effect.

How It's Done:

1. **Draw with Crayons:**
   - Use white or light-coloured crayons to draw on white watercolour paper.
   - Create patterns, write messages, or make simple drawings.
2. **Prepare Watercolours:**
   - Set up watercolour paints and brushes.
3. **Paint Over the Drawing:**
   - Brush watercolour paint over the entire paper.
   - Watch as the crayon resist reveals the hidden design.
4. **Experiment with Colours:**
   - Use multiple paint colours for a vibrant effect.
   - Layer different resist drawings.

Benefits:

- **Artistic Expression:** Encourages creativity and experimentation.
- **Fine Motor Skills:** Drawing and painting enhance coordination.
- **Understanding Materials:** Explores how different mediums interact.
- **Sensory Experience:** Engages sight and touch.

Toys and Tools Used:

- **Watercolour Paper**
- **Crayons**
- **Watercolour Paints and Brushes**

This activity can be themed for holidays, seasons, or educational topics. It's suitable for various ages and allows for open-ended creativity.

182. Learning Sign Language Basics

Introduce **Basic Sign Language** to enhance communication skills. Learning simple signs can be fun and beneficial for all children.

How It's Done:

1. **Choose Resources:**
   - Use books, flashcards, or online videos designed for children.
2. **Start with Simple Signs:**
   - Teach signs for common words like "eat," "more," "please," "thank you," "yes," "no."
3. **Practice Regularly:**
   - Incorporate signs into daily routines.
   - Encourage repetition and use in context.
4. **Make It Fun:**
   - Learn songs in sign language.
   - Play games that involve signing.

Benefits:

- **Communication Skills:** Expands ways to express needs and thoughts.
- **Cognitive Development:** Enhances memory and language processing.
- **Inclusivity:** Promotes understanding of different communication methods.
- **Fine Motor Skills:** Signing improves hand coordination.

Toys and Tools Used:

- **Educational Materials:** Books, flashcards, videos.
- **Interactive Activities:** Songs, games.

Learning sign language can be particularly helpful for non-verbal children or those with speech delays. It's an inclusive activity that fosters empathy and social awareness.

---

183. Cloud Watching and Storytelling

Engage in **Cloud Watching** to stimulate imagination and relaxation. This simple activity involves observing clouds and creating stories based on their shapes.

How It's Done:

1. **Find a Comfortable Spot:**
   - Lay out a blanket in a safe outdoor area.
2. **Observe the Clouds:**
   - Look up and notice different cloud formations.
3. **Create Stories:**
   - Identify shapes resembling animals, objects, or characters.
   - Invent stories or descriptions based on the cloud shapes.
4. **Discuss Weather (Optional):**
   - Talk about different types of clouds and weather patterns.

Benefits:

- **Imagination:** Encourages creative thinking and storytelling.
- **Relaxation:** Provides a calming and mindful experience.
- **Environmental Awareness:** Connects with nature and weather.
- **Language Development:** Enhances descriptive vocabulary.

Toys and Tools Used:

- **Blanket or Mat**
- **Outdoor Space**

This activity requires no materials and can be a spontaneous way to enjoy the outdoors. It's suitable for all ages and can be a shared experience with family or friends.

184. DIY Scratch Art

Create **DIY Scratch Art** to reveal colourful designs beneath a surface layer. This craft combines creativity with a tactile experience.

How It's Done:

1. **Prepare the Base:**
   - Colour a piece of cardstock or heavy paper completely with bright crayons.
   - Ensure the entire surface is covered.
2. **Apply the Top Layer:**
   - Mix black tempera paint with a few drops of dish soap.
   - Paint over the crayon layer completely.
   - Allow it to dry thoroughly.
3. **Scratch Your Design:**
   - Use a wooden stylus, toothpick, or blunt object to scratch away the black layer.
   - Reveal the colourful layer beneath with drawings or patterns.

Benefits:

- **Artistic Expression:** Encourages creativity and design.
- **Fine Motor Skills:** Scratching requires precision and control.
- **Sensory Experience:** Provides tactile feedback.
- **Understanding Layers:** Introduces concepts of layering and contrast.

Toys and Tools Used:

- **Cardstock or Heavy Paper**
- **Crayons and Black Tempera Paint**
- **Dish Soap**
- **Scratching Tool:** Stylus, toothpick.

Ensure the scratching tool is safe and appropriate for the child's age. This activity can be themed for holidays or personal interests, and the finished artwork can be displayed or gifted.

185. Nature Collage with Collected Items

Create a **Nature Collage** using items collected from the outdoors, such as leaves, twigs, flowers, and seeds. This activity encourages exploration of nature and artistic expression.

How It's Done:

1. **Collect Materials:**
   o Go on a nature walk and gather various natural items.
   o Ensure that collected items are safe and not from protected areas.
2. **Prepare the Base:**
   o Use cardboard, poster board, or thick paper as the collage base.
3. **Design the Collage:**
   o Arrange the natural items on the base to create a picture or abstract design.
   o Experiment with different layouts before gluing.
4. **Attach the Items:**
   o Use glue or double-sided tape to secure the items to the base.
   o Press firmly to ensure they stick.
5. **Optional Additions:**
   o Label the items with their names.
   o Add drawings or paint to enhance the collage.

Benefits:

- **Connection with Nature:** Fosters appreciation for the environment.
- **Fine Motor Skills:** Handling small items improves dexterity.
- **Creative Expression:** Encourages artistic creativity.
- **Sensory Exploration:** Engages touch and sight.

Toys and Tools Used:

- **Natural Materials:** Leaves, twigs, flowers.
- **Base Material:** Cardboard or thick paper.
- **Glue or Tape**
- **Optional:** Markers, labels.

Discuss the importance of respecting nature by only taking what is needed and avoiding harm to plants and animals. This activity can be themed around seasons or specific habitats.

186. Bubble Wrap Roadway

Create a **Bubble Wrap Roadway** for toy cars and vehicles. The textured surface adds sensory input and makes playtime more engaging.

How It's Done:

1. **Prepare the Bubble Wrap:**
   o Lay out a long piece of bubble wrap on the floor.
   o Secure it with tape to prevent slipping.
2. **Design the Road:**
   o Use markers to draw roads, intersections, and parking spaces on the bubble wrap.
   o Add signs or decorations if desired.
3. **Play with Vehicles:**
   o Provide toy cars, trucks, or trains.
   o Encourage your child to drive the vehicles along the roads.
4. **Enhance the Experience:**
   o Incorporate obstacles or ramps.
   o Pop the bubbles by driving over them for auditory feedback.

Benefits:

- **Sensory Stimulation:** Popping bubbles provides tactile and auditory input.
- **Fine Motor Skills:** Manipulating vehicles improves coordination.
- **Creative Play:** Encourages imaginative scenarios.
- **Visual Tracking:** Following moving vehicles enhances visual skills.

Toys and Tools Used:

- **Bubble Wrap**
- **Tape and Markers**
- **Toy Vehicles**

Ensure the bubble wrap is safe for play and supervise to prevent slipping. This activity combines sensory exploration with traditional play.

187. Chalk Shadow Tracing

Use sidewalk chalk to **Trace Shadows** of objects or people, exploring light and shadow while creating unique artworks.

How It's Done:

1. **Choose a Sunny Day:**
   - Select a time when shadows are prominent, like early morning or late afternoon.
2. **Select Objects:**
   - Use toys, plants, or have someone stand to cast a shadow.
3. **Trace the Shadows:**
   - Outline the shadow on the pavement with chalk.
   - Fill in the traced shape with colours or patterns.
4. **Observe Changes:**
   - Return after some time to see how the shadow has moved.
   - Discuss how the sun's position affects shadows.

Benefits:

- **Scientific Exploration:** Introduces concepts of light, shadows, and time.
- **Artistic Expression:** Encourages creativity in decorating traced shapes.
- **Gross Motor Skills:** Involves movement and coordination.
- **Environmental Awareness:** Connects with natural phenomena.

Toys and Tools Used:

- **Sidewalk Chalk**
- **Objects or Participants to Cast Shadows**
- **Open Pavement Area**

This activity can lead to discussions about the Earth's rotation and the concept of time. It's a simple way to combine science and art.

188. Pasta Necklace Craft

Make a **Pasta Necklace** by threading dyed pasta onto string. This craft enhances fine motor skills and allows for creative expression.

How It's Done:

1. **Dye the Pasta (Optional):**
   - Place uncooked pasta shapes (like penne or macaroni) in ziplock bags.
   - Add a few drops of food colouring and a teaspoon of rubbing alcohol.
   - Shake until evenly coated and let dry.
2. **Prepare the String:**
   - Cut a piece of yarn or string to the desired length.
   - Tape one end to make threading easier.
3. **Thread the Pasta:**
   - Encourage your child to string the pasta onto the yarn.
   - Create patterns with colours and shapes.
4. **Finish the Necklace:**
   - Tie the ends together securely.
   - Wear or display the necklace.

Benefits:

- **Fine Motor Skills:** Threading enhances hand-eye coordination.
- **Pattern Recognition:** Arranging colours and shapes promotes cognitive skills.
- **Creative Expression:** Personalizing the necklace fosters creativity.
- **Sensory Play:** Handling pasta provides tactile stimulation.

Toys and Tools Used:

- **Uncooked Pasta**
- **Food Colouring (Optional)**
- **Yarn or String**
- **Ziplock Bags**

Ensure that pasta pieces are large enough to prevent choking hazards. This activity can be adapted by using beads or other threading materials.

---

189. DIY Bird Watching Station

Set up a **Bird Watching Station** to observe and learn about local bird species. This activity promotes patience, observation, and connection with nature.

How It's Done:

1. **Create a Feeding Area:**
   o Hang bird feeders filled with appropriate seed.
   o Place feeders near windows for easy viewing.
2. **Prepare Observation Tools:**
   o Provide binoculars (child-friendly versions).
   o Use a notebook for recording sightings.
3. **Learn About Birds:**
   o Use field guides or apps to identify different species.
   o Note characteristics like colours, sizes, and songs.
4. **Maintain the Station:**
   o Keep feeders clean and filled.
   o Observe regularly to see different birds.

Benefits:

- **Environmental Education:** Teaches about wildlife and ecosystems.
- **Observation Skills:** Enhances attention to detail.
- **Patience and Mindfulness:** Encourages quiet observation.
- **Scientific Inquiry:** Introduces data recording and species identification.

Toys and Tools Used:

- **Bird Feeders and Seed**
- **Binoculars**
- **Notebook and Field Guides**

Respect wildlife by providing appropriate food and not disturbing nesting areas. This activity can become a long-term hobby and foster a love for nature.

---

190. Sensory Play with Cornmeal

Use **Cornmeal** in a sensory bin for a unique tactile experience. Cornmeal's fine texture provides a different sensation compared to sand or rice.

How It's Done:

1. **Set Up the Sensory Bin:**
   - Fill a large container with cornmeal.
   - Ensure the play area is easy to clean.
2. **Add Tools and Toys:**
   - Include scoops, funnels, measuring cups, and small toys.
   - Hide objects for a treasure hunt.
3. **Engage in Play:**
   - Encourage your child to explore the texture.
   - Practice pouring, scooping, and measuring.
4. **Incorporate Learning:**
   - Draw letters or shapes in the cornmeal.
   - Discuss concepts like volume and weight.

Benefits:

- **Tactile Sensory Input:** Fine texture stimulates touch.
- **Fine Motor Skills:** Handling tools improves coordination.
- **Cognitive Development:** Introduces mathematical concepts.
- **Creative Play:** Open-ended exploration fosters imagination.

Toys and Tools Used:

- **Cornmeal**
- **Container or Sensory Bin**
- **Utensils:** Scoops, cups, funnels.
- **Small Toys**

Monitor play to prevent ingestion, especially with younger children. Cornmeal can be reused if stored properly.

191. Origami Folding

Introduce **Origami**, the art of paper folding, to create various shapes and figures. This activity enhances fine motor skills and concentration.

How It's Done:

1. **Choose Simple Models:**
   - Start with basic shapes like boats, airplanes, or animals.
2. **Provide Instructions:**
   - Use step-by-step diagrams, videos, or books.
3. **Practice Folding:**
   - Guide your child through each fold.
   - Encourage patience and precision.
4. **Decorate the Creations:**
   - Add eyes, patterns, or colours with markers.

Benefits:

- **Fine Motor Skills:** Precise folding improves dexterity.
- **Cognitive Development:** Follows sequences and instructions.
- **Creative Expression:** Personalizing models fosters creativity.
- **Cultural Education:** Introduces aspects of Japanese culture.

Toys and Tools Used:

- **Origami Paper or Square Paper**
- **Instructional Materials**
- **Markers or Decorations**

Origami can range from simple to complex, allowing for progression as skills improve. It's a portable activity suitable for quiet times.

192. Sound Walk Exploration

Take a **Sound Walk** to focus on auditory sensations in different environments. This activity enhances listening skills and environmental awareness.

How It's Done:

1. **Plan the Walk:**

- Choose different locations like a park, city street, or near water.
2. **Set the Intent:**
   - Explain that the goal is to listen carefully to all the sounds.
3. **During the Walk:**
   - Pause periodically to focus on specific sounds.
   - Identify sources like birds, traffic, water, or wind.
4. **Document the Sounds:**
   - Use a notebook to write down or draw what was heard.
   - Optionally, record sounds with a device.

Benefits:

- **Auditory Discrimination:** Enhances ability to distinguish sounds.
- **Mindfulness:** Encourages presence and focus.
- **Language Development:** Expands descriptive vocabulary.
- **Emotional Regulation:** Can be calming and grounding.

Toys and Tools Used:

- **Notebook and Pen**
- **Recording Device (Optional)**

Discuss the importance of quiet and active listening. This activity can be repeated in various settings to compare and contrast sounds.

193. Building a Mini Greenhouse

Construct a **Mini Greenhouse** using recycled materials to learn about plant growth and ecosystems.

How It's Done:

1. **Gather Materials:**
   - Use a clear plastic container with a lid or a plastic bottle cut in half.
   - Obtain potting soil and seeds.
2. **Plant the Seeds:**
   - Fill the container with soil.
   - Plant seeds according to instructions.

3. **Create the Greenhouse Effect:**
    - Cover the container with its lid or the top half of the bottle.
    - Place in a sunny spot.
4. **Monitor Growth:**
    - Observe condensation and how the greenhouse retains moisture.
    - Record growth progress.

Benefits:

- **Scientific Learning:** Teaches about plant biology and greenhouse effects.
- **Responsibility:** Caring for plants fosters accountability.
- **Observation Skills:** Enhances attention to detail.
- **Recycling Awareness:** Utilizes recycled materials.

Toys and Tools Used:

- **Clear Plastic Container or Bottle**
- **Potting Soil and Seeds**
- **Watering Tool**

Choose fast-growing seeds for quicker results. This project can lead to discussions about sustainability and environmental conservation.

194. Texture Painting with Unusual Tools

Explore art by **Texture Painting** using unconventional tools like sponges, toothbrushes, or combs. This activity stimulates creativity and sensory exploration.

How It's Done:

1. **Prepare Materials:**
    - Use washable paints and thick paper.
    - Gather tools like sponges, feathers, forks, or bubble wrap.
2. **Experiment with Textures:**
    - Dip tools into paint and apply to paper.
    - Observe the different patterns and effects.

3. **Create a Masterpiece:**
    - Encourage layering and combining textures.
    - Allow freedom to explore and make abstract art.
4. **Discuss the Process:**
    - Talk about how each tool creates a unique texture.
    - Encourage describing sensations and preferences.

Benefits:

- **Sensory Stimulation:** Engages touch and sight.
- **Fine Motor Skills:** Handling various tools enhances coordination.
- **Creative Expression:** Fosters artistic experimentation.
- **Language Development:** Describing textures expands vocabulary.

Toys and Tools Used:

- **Washable Paints**
- **Paper**
- **Unconventional Tools:** Sponges, combs, forks.

Protect the work area with a drop cloth. This activity allows for open-ended creativity and can be adapted for all ages.

---

195. Nature Journal Keeping

Encourage observation and reflection by **Keeping a Nature Journal**. Documenting experiences in nature enhances mindfulness and writing skills.

How It's Done:

1. **Provide a Journal:**
    - Use a notebook or create a homemade journal.
2. **Set Intentions:**
    - Explain that the journal is for recording observations, thoughts, and drawings related to nature.
3. **Explore Outdoors:**
    - Go for walks or spend time in the backyard.
4. **Document Experiences:**

- o Write descriptions of sights, sounds, and feelings.
- o Include sketches or attach collected items like leaves.

Benefits:

- **Writing Skills:** Enhances descriptive writing and expression.
- **Mindfulness:** Encourages presence and reflection.
- **Artistic Expression:** Drawing and sketching improve creativity.
- **Environmental Awareness:** Deepens connection with nature.

Toys and Tools Used:

- **Journal or Notebook**
- **Writing and Drawing Supplies**

Review the journal together to discuss observations. This activity can be a long-term project, fostering continuous engagement with nature.

196. Sensory Play with Feathers

Use **Feathers** for a soft and gentle sensory experience. This activity provides tactile stimulation and can be calming.

How It's Done:

1. **Gather Feathers:**
   - o Use craft feathers in various colours and sizes.
   - o Ensure they are clean and safe for play.
2. **Set Up the Play Area:**
   - o Place feathers in a shallow bin or on a soft surface.
3. **Engage in Play:**
   - o Encourage your child to touch, sort, and move the feathers.
   - o Blow feathers into the air to watch them float.
4. **Incorporate Learning:**
   - o Discuss colours, sizes, and textures.
   - o Count feathers or create patterns.

Benefits:

- **Tactile Sensory Input:** Soft texture stimulates touch.
- **Fine Motor Skills:** Picking up and manipulating feathers improves dexterity.
- **Calming Activity:** Gentle play can reduce stress.
- **Language Development:** Expands descriptive vocabulary.

Toys and Tools Used:

- **Craft Feathers**
- **Container or Soft Surface**

Supervise to prevent feathers from being mouthed by younger children. This activity can be combined with crafts like making feather collages.

---

197. Making Homemade Ice Cream in a Bag

Enjoy a tasty science experiment by making **Homemade Ice Cream in a Bag**. This activity combines cooking, science, and sensory experiences.

How It's Done:

1. **Prepare Ingredients:**
   - Half-and-half or milk, sugar, vanilla extract.
   - Ice, rock salt.
2. **Mix the Ice Cream Base:**
   - In a small ziplock bag, combine 1 cup half-and-half, 2 tablespoons sugar, and 1/2 teaspoon vanilla.
   - Seal the bag tightly.
3. **Prepare the Ice Bag:**
   - In a larger ziplock bag, place ice and 1/2 cup of rock salt.
4. **Combine and Shake:**
   - Place the small bag inside the large bag.
   - Seal the large bag and shake vigorously for 5-10 minutes.
5. **Enjoy the Ice Cream:**
   - Remove the small bag, rinse off saltwater, and serve.

Benefits:

- **Scientific Understanding:** Teaches about freezing points and state changes.
- **Physical Activity:** Shaking the bag involves movement.
- **Sensory Experience:** Engages taste, touch, and sight.
- **Cooking Skills:** Introduces measuring and following instructions.

Toys and Tools Used:

- **Ziplock Bags (Small and Large)**
- **Ingredients:** Half-and-half, sugar, vanilla, ice, rock salt.
- **Measuring Cups and Spoons**

Ensure bags are sealed properly to prevent leaks. This activity can be adapted with different flavors by adding cocoa powder or fruit puree.

198. Balloon Rockets

Demonstrate principles of physics by making **Balloon Rockets** that zoom along a string. This activity is exciting and educational.

How It's Done:

1. **Set Up the Rocket Path:**
   o Thread a long piece of string through a straw.
   o Tie each end of the string to sturdy supports, keeping it taut.
2. **Prepare the Balloon:**
   o Inflate a balloon but do not tie it.
   o Pinch the end to hold the air.
3. **Attach the Balloon:**
   o Tape the balloon to the straw.
4. **Launch the Rocket:**
   o Release the balloon and watch it propel along the string.
5. **Experiment:**
   o Try different balloon sizes.
   o Adjust the angle of the string.

Benefits:

- **Scientific Learning:** Introduces concepts of propulsion and air pressure.
- **Problem-Solving:** Encourages experimentation.
- **Fine Motor Skills:** Handling balloons and tape improves coordination.
- **Excitement and Engagement:** Provides a fun, dynamic activity.

Toys and Tools Used:

- **Balloons**
- **String and Straw**
- **Tape**
- **Supports:** Chairs, doorknobs.

Discuss how the air escaping the balloon propels it forward. This activity can be expanded into lessons about Newton's laws of motion.

199. Making Friendship Bracelets

Craft **Friendship Bracelets** using colourful threads. This activity promotes fine motor skills and can be a social bonding experience.

How It's Done:

1. **Select Embroidery Floss:**
   - Choose multiple colours.
2. **Prepare the Threads:**
   - Cut equal lengths (about 24 inches each).
   - Knot them together at one end.
3. **Create the Bracelet:**
   - Use simple knotting techniques like the forward knot.
   - Follow patterns or create your own.
4. **Finish and Share:**
   - Tie the bracelet onto a wrist.
   - Make bracelets for friends or family.

Benefits:

- **Fine Motor Skills:** Knotting enhances dexterity.
- **Pattern Recognition:** Following patterns develops cognitive skills.

- **Social Connection:** Sharing bracelets fosters relationships.
- **Creative Expression:** Choosing colours and designs encourages creativity.

Toys and Tools Used:

- **Embroidery Floss or Thread**
- **Scissors**
- **Tape or Clipboard:** To hold threads in place.

Begin with simple patterns and progress to more complex ones. This activity can be a part of cultural education, discussing the history of friendship bracelets.

---

200. Sensory Play with Kinetic Sand

Explore **Kinetic Sand**, a moldable sand that sticks to itself but not to hands. This sensory material provides a unique tactile experience.

How It's Done:

1. **Obtain Kinetic Sand:**
   - Purchase from a store or make homemade kinetic sand using sand, cornstarch, and oil.
2. **Set Up the Play Area:**
   - Place sand in a large bin or tray.
3. **Provide Tools:**
   - Include molds, cookie cutters, and utensils.
4. **Engage in Play:**
   - Encourage squeezing, molding, and cutting the sand.
   - Build structures or simply enjoy the texture.

Benefits:

- **Tactile Sensory Input:** Engages touch with a unique feel.
- **Fine Motor Skills:** Manipulating sand strengthens hand muscles.
- **Creative Play:** Open-ended exploration fosters imagination.
- **Calming Activity:** Can reduce stress and anxiety.

Toys and Tools Used:

- **Kinetic Sand**
- **Container**
- **Molds and Utensils**

Kinetic sand is easy to clean up as it sticks together. Store in an airtight container to keep it fresh. This activity is suitable for various ages and abilities.

---

201. Leaf Printing Art

Create **Leaf Prints** by painting leaves and pressing them onto paper. This art activity captures natural patterns and textures.

How It's Done:

1. **Collect Leaves:**
   - Choose leaves with interesting shapes and veins.
2. **Prepare Materials:**
   - Use washable paints and brushes.
   - Have paper or canvas ready.
3. **Apply Paint:**
   - Paint the underside of the leaf where veins are prominent.
4. **Press onto Paper:**
   - Place the painted side down on the paper.
   - Press gently and then lift to reveal the print.
5. **Experiment with Colours:**
   - Use different paint colours.
   - Layer prints for a collage effect.

Benefits:

- **Artistic Expression:** Encourages creativity.
- **Fine Motor Skills:** Painting and pressing enhance coordination.
- **Nature Appreciation:** Connects art with the natural world.
- **Sensory Experience:** Engages touch and sight.

Toys and Tools Used:

- **Leaves**

- **Paints and Brushes**
- **Paper or Canvas**

This activity can be tied to lessons about plants and seasons. Ensure leaves are clean and safe to use.

---

202. Making a Rainstick Instrument

Craft a **Rainstick**, a percussion instrument that mimics the sound of falling rain. This project combines art, music, and sensory exploration.

How It's Done:

1. **Gather Materials:**
   - Use a cardboard tube (like a paper towel roll).
   - Obtain small nails or toothpicks, rice or beans, and decorative materials.
2. **Assemble the Rainstick:**
   - Push nails or toothpicks through the tube in a spiral pattern.
   - Seal one end with paper and tape.
3. **Add Fillings:**
   - Pour rice or beans into the tube.
   - Seal the other end securely.
4. **Decorate:**
   - Wrap with paper, paint, or add stickers.
5. **Explore Sounds:**
   - Tilt the rainstick to hear the sound of rain.
   - Experiment with different fillings for varied sounds.

Benefits:

- **Auditory Sensory Input:** Produces soothing sounds.
- **Fine Motor Skills:** Building the instrument enhances coordination.
- **Creative Expression:** Decorating allows artistic freedom.
- **Cultural Education:** Introduces instruments from different cultures.

Toys and Tools Used:

- **Cardboard Tube**
- **Nails or Toothpicks**
- **Rice or Beans**
- **Decorative Supplies**

Supervise the use of sharp objects during assembly. This activity can lead to discussions about music, weather, and cultural traditions.

203. String Art Designs

Create **String Art** by wrapping colourful threads around pins on a board to form geometric patterns or images.

How It's Done:

1. **Prepare the Base:**
   - Use a wooden board or thick foam board.
   - Draw a simple design or pattern.
2. **Insert Pins or Nails:**
   - Hammer small nails along the design lines, spaced evenly.
   - Alternatively, use pushpins for foam boards.
3. **Wrap the String:**
   - Tie the string to one nail and weave it around the nails to fill the design.
   - Use different colours for effect.
4. **Finish and Display:**
   - Secure the end of the string.
   - Hang or display the artwork.

Benefits:

- **Fine Motor Skills:** Wrapping string requires precision.
- **Artistic Expression:** Encourages creativity in design and colour choice.
- **Math Skills:** Understanding geometric patterns.
- **Concentration:** Requires focus and planning.

Toys and Tools Used:

- **Board:** Wood or foam.
- **Nails or Pins**
- **String or Embroidery Floss**
- **Hammer (if using nails)**

Choose simple designs to start, like hearts or stars. Always supervise when using tools. This activity is suitable for older children who can handle small parts and tools safely.

---

204. Making a Solar Oven

Construct a **Solar Oven** to cook simple foods using the sun's energy. This activity teaches about renewable energy and science.

How It's Done:

1. **Prepare Materials:**
   - Use a pizza box, aluminum foil, plastic wrap, black construction paper, and tape.
2. **Assemble the Oven:**
   - Cut a flap in the lid of the pizza box.
   - Line the flap and inside of the box with aluminum foil.
   - Place black paper at the bottom.
   - Cover the opening with plastic wrap to create an airtight window.
3. **Position the Oven:**
   - Angle the foil-lined flap to reflect sunlight into the box.
   - Secure with a stick or ruler.
4. **Cook Simple Foods:**
   - Place s'mores, nachos, or hot dogs inside.
   - Allow time for the food to heat and cook.
5. **Monitor and Enjoy:**
   - Check periodically.
   - Enjoy the cooked food.

Benefits:

- **Scientific Learning:** Teaches about solar energy and heat transfer.
- **Environmental Awareness:** Introduces renewable energy concepts.

- **Problem-Solving:** Building the oven involves planning.
- **Cooking Skills:** Simple food preparation.

Toys and Tools Used:

- **Pizza Box**
- **Aluminum Foil**
- **Plastic Wrap**
- **Black Paper**
- **Tape and Scissors**

This activity requires a sunny day and patience. Always handle hot items with care. It's an engaging way to combine science and practical skills.

Made in the USA
Columbia, SC
27 November 2024

47761631R00130